# WHAT DID YOU DO IN THE WAR, DADDY?

# WHAT
# DID YOU DO
# IN THE WAR,
# DADDY?

## *Growing Up German*

## Sabine Reichel, 1946-

*Hill and Wang*

NEW YORK

Library of Congress Cataloging-in-Publication Data
Reichel, Sabine
What did you do in the war, Daddy?
1. Reichel, Sabine.  2. Germany—History—
1933–1945.  3. National socialism.  4. Guilt.  5. German
Americans—Biography.  I. Title.
DD256.5.R45  1989     943.086'092'4     88-32821

Chapter 3, "What Did You Do in the War, Daddy?" was
originally published, in different form, as "Tell Me About the
Nazis, Daddy" in *The Village Voice*, May 10, 1983. Chapter 8,
"Third Reich Reunion," was originally published, in slightly
different form, as "What Did You Do in the War, Daddy?" in
*Rolling Stone*, March 31, 1983.

# Contents

*You who will emerge from the flood*
*In which we have gone under*
*Remember*
*When you speak of our failings*
*The dark time too*
*Which you have escaped.*
    —Bertolt Brecht,
      from "To Those Born Later"

# WHAT
# DID YOU DO
# IN THE WAR,
# DADDY?

# Spying on the Home Front:
# An Introduction

It still isn't fun to be German. It's a bit like having a genetic disease for which a cure hasn't been found. Once in a while when a plucky New York cabdriver asks me, "Where are you from?" I snap back with a curt and icy "Why?"— as if revealing my nationality were an act of treason or could be used against me. History is a mean slasher. It lurks somewhere in the dark, crawls up to you surreptitiously, and lashes out. History hurts and haunts, leaving invisible scars, even on smooth, pink baby skin. But sooner or later they burst open. A Nazi war criminal is caught, a moving account of a spirited Jewish woman who perished in a concentration camp is discovered, a photo of vile men in riding pants shoving children into cattle cars is printed somewhere . . . and I feel personally accused. In these moments I hate Germany.

"Leave our children out of this, they're innocent," said my father to the first American troops he met in Austria in the spring of 1945. I don't know what they answered but

I do know that his plea didn't work. Sorry, Dad, but guilt
can be a feeling, not a fact, and referring to my age never
relieved me from the burden of my father's generation.
"Here ends the civilized world. You are entering Germany. Fraternizing prohibited," read Allied signs all over
the country in 1945. Nice description for a fatherland. I
was born right after the end of civilization and raised among
uncommonly uncivilized ruins, in 1946, in Hamburg—a
German girl in a worthless land, an heir to an inescapable,
unwanted legacy for which I was never prepared. And what
had my Nazi predecessors left me for a birthday present?
A junkyard of a country, a fallow, barren wasteland, sundered and soaked with blood, its spirit suffocated by the
dead souls of the people who were killed with a fierce hand
and a light heart. It was a place with black shadows that
could suddenly swallow you up. I was placed right where
they could dump the detritus of a "Thousand-Year Reich"
on my head and was expected to find my way in their
ravaged world without instructions, groping in the dark for
some identity. Who are you when you have no faith in your
fatherland, no love for your countrymen, when your roots
are chopped off to a stump without hope of regeneration
because the soil is poisoned?

Even to this day I feel Germany's depressing aura of being
hermetically sealed off from the rest of the world. A country
trapped in unaccepted guilt where the Nazi past covers the
natives like an adhesive coat of a corrosive material that
makes you want to peel your skin off. I tried to tear myself
away from that stifling legacy, almost violently. But like
freckles and crooked teeth, it stayed with me.

You watch TV, it can be 1965, 1972, 1989. You see
footage of Auschwitz and the liberation of Dachau, your
eyes fill with tears, your stomach contracts, you look at

your father if he happens to be sitting next to you, and if not, you think of him—and you curse your relationship to him. You want to scream, hide, tear your genes out, burn your passport, be a Martian instead of being part of these terrible people, but all you are is a helplessly German daughter with nowhere to hide.

How was it, I later asked myself, that I had never consciously delved into a past that loomed so large over the present? How had I managed over the years to simply erase that subject from my mind without ever noticing it? Complicated forces must have been at work, more powerful and effective than mind-altering drugs. We postwar children were all injected with an overdose of a conscience killer long before we could think independently. When Nazi Germany finally collapsed and the truth couldn't be denied anymore, the demoralized Germans made a peace treaty with their souls for a new start: There would be no discussion of that shameful past, no analyzing, no reflecting, no mourning, and no regretting. There would be no need for answers because there would be no questions.

The zero hour started with that fatal pact, and when the war was over the forgetting began by a legion of shattered and defeated people, determined not to let repentance and sorrow obstruct their newly concocted happiness that was as meretricious as the golden calf. It was impossible for the Germans not to respond to a shocked world, and to interrogations and trials (God knows they tried), but their children were born innocent. We couldn't pass judgment. We hadn't witnessed the nation's march toward destruction, hadn't heard the Führer's venomous tirades, hadn't seen the ecstatic faces screaming "*Heil!*" and the smiling faces of the SS by the trenches saying "Shoot." We didn't yet know about genocide and gas chambers, ramps and cattle cars with destinations like Auschwitz and Treblinka, Majdanek and Dachau. Everything was scrupulously prepared for the omission of a traumatic chapter. The curiosity for certain subjects was simply bred out of us, conveniently and without fingerprints: the perfect crime. But it was the beginning of a life laced with deep mistrust and feelings of shame. By using their children in this way, our parents created the illusion of doing something noble under the pretext of protecting us, whereas they were really protecting themselves. An offspring with a powerful future who didn't look back began to grow up in Germany.

The stratagem was superficially successful. Most of the evidence was erased. When I grew up, nothing reminded us of the Nazi past. Together with the Führer, the swastikas, the Jews, and the "Adolf-Hitler-Platz" street signs, the memory of a whole country disappeared in a bout of amnesia and was replaced by a calamitous silence. By the time I became aware of Nazi crimes by way of infrequent TV documentaries, superficial history lessons, and the occasional magazine article and story shown to me by my father, I still didn't want to know the perpetrators. I sensed danger.

For me, that generation which my father was part of was always *them*—contemptible aliens whom I regarded as cripples. Their handicap was their past, and for the longest time I treated them the way I was taught to respond to the disabled, by courteously pretending to overlook their deformity. The Germans, paragons of immaculate living, were really imperfect creatures with cracks and holes in a surface that, no matter how artfully mended, could never be restored to its former splendor in spite of exhausting efforts; this I realized by the time I was sixteen. Yet even in my late twenties I still wasn't fully aware of how historically significant the older people around me were, and what explosive ballast they carried with them. In fact, I was surrounded by the entire alumni of the Third Reich. Can anybody understand the experience of growing up among people with such a gruesome past? People who looked like a kindhearted, friendly neighbor or a trustworthy politician perhaps were once "just doing their duty." Is it possible to look at an elderly German today without thinking, "I wonder what kind of orders he carried out?" My dislike for them was based mostly on gut feelings and real-life encounters. I didn't feel the need to know details about their lives in order to condemn them. By the time I was a young adolescent I had collected enough emotional evidence to declare them my enemy, mainly because they, then in their early fifties, were still setting the tone of Germany's political culture.

As I grew older, they grew older and that was a disaster. They turned into an army of cane-swinging, sour-faced, complaining pensioners whose inconspicuous and benign appearance belied the danger and brutality for which they were once feared by the whole world. The cadenced goose step in shiny black jackboots was replaced by scuffling feet in well-worn brown crepe-soled shoes, the flat stomachs covered by a stupendous variety of black or brown uniforms were now beer bellies tucked away under powder-blue jersey shirts. Little crunched hats were perched atop the still neatly trimmed hair where once the sharp and scary high-brimmed headgear sat. Gold-framed glasses in front of squinting, suspicious eyes completed the picture of a large survivors' club whose compulsory dress code had taken a radical turn from military pomp to polyester. All in all, they looked not unlike the image of nasty, piggish-looking Prussians, the way George Grosz had depicted his countrymen after World War I, before he was banned by the Nazis as a "decadent" artist.

I remember my first public encounter with one of these senior citizens as if it were today. It was on the Reeperbahn in Hamburg, a favorite launching pad for the countless British "beat groups" who came over by boat in search of enthusiastic audiences and hard Deutschmarks, hoping to duplicate the Beatles' legendary success. The year was 1968, and I was with a friend who was shooting a documentary about the Spencer Davis Group, then touring Germany. While we stood talking to the musicians, who sported nothing bolder than white patent-leather shoes, shirts with paisley prints, pipe pants, and hair that barely covered their necks, an older man who had been giving us dirty looks approached us. "Who are these filthy, long-haired rats?" he said to no one in particular. I was torn between wanting to tear his tongue out and sinking two hundred feet underground. Blood rushed to my head as I yelled "Shut up!" at the top of my lungs, hoping to silence him before he could continue. I glanced at the musicians to check their reaction. They seemed to be mildly amused, and less shocked by the man than by my violent outburst. Foreigners expect Nazis to be lurking everywhere in Germany, I thought—and they are right.

"We need Hitler back, that's what we need," the man insisted. "In the Third Reich this wouldn't be allowed. Such elements belong in the gas chambers or should work hard for a change. Compulsory labor is the thing for all of you," he assured us, adding that Adolf himself would have handled things a bit more radically.

I had witnessed several such outspoken requests for the beloved Führer's presence by older men and women—but this was different. These were foreigners, friends, idols,

British musicians who represented my favorite culture and language; I wanted to be liked and accepted by them. What was worse, my English friends couldn't defend themselves verbally, they were once again being made victims.

"Damned Nazi pig," I swore, and walked toward him, head on fire. I hated him, hated Germany, hated being German. He and I spoke the same language. I was ashamed, embarrassed, and humiliated and so full of anger that I might have attacked him if he hadn't chosen to walk away at that moment. Here, in front of foreigners, this pesky old German had once again destroyed my hope of forgetting where I came from. He exposed my legacy and stripped me naked.

There was an uncomfortable silence. The few Germans in the group seemed shaken. Should we apologize for being Germans and reassure our English visitors that we were really different? But that was understood, wasn't it? The British, on the other hand, with typical understatement, didn't take the incident so seriously; they were all sympathetic smiles and understanding looks. Sure, they had nothing to worry about, they were English. I envied them for that.

Had I overreacted? Was I too sensitive, too willing to blow trivial incidents out of proportion, simply paranoid when confronted by conservative right-wingers who no longer posed any serious threat to an otherwise truly democratic nation? American friends would later reassure me, "Look, we had the same experiences with people like that here in the sixties. They said the same things to us, hated us, wanted to get rid of us." They couldn't have said the same things. It isn't the same, can't be the same, and maybe only a German my age can understand that. Of course, one doesn't have to be a former Nazi to heap abuse on minorities who don't fit in. But nowhere in the world does a generation have to come to terms with a more devastating historical crime than we do in Germany.

I left Germany without sadness when I moved to New York in 1975. Was I glad to have escaped! But being away from Germany had an unexpected effect on me. Slowly the past caught up with me. I began to realize that I still didn't know exactly what my father did in the war. Like a boomerang that had gotten lost for twenty years and had only now decided to come back and hit me in the head, my father and his generation struck me as precious eyewitnesses who had to be confronted before they all died and escaped from me again—forever.

My motives were anything but noble. It wasn't the historian in me that needed to come to terms with the past, but anger and outrage against people who had betrayed me by their silence, crippling me by their refusal to speak. They had failed as parents and teachers, now I felt they owed me an encounter and I would make them talk—face to face.

What did I want from them? No confessions. I wanted to fill the vacuum in my head, grab a piece of the past, just for myself, and for that I had to involve myself physically and mentally. Back to Germany, back to the source of the pain. Psychoanalysis on a nation's couch. My mission: soul espionage. I felt like an archaeologist excavating a rare find, a detective in search of a lost time and the missing conscience of a country. Detectives need disguises. I used the one I was born with. Being a young woman with seemingly innocent questions, I wasn't a threat to the old warriors whose minds were never troubled by thoughts about the possible existence of the female brain. My act as a well-behaved, demure, and unpretentious "ersatz" daughter was well received and brought out the jovial and paternalistic side in them. I was also German. Choosing people to interview was easy: I could approach any older-looking stranger—on the street, in parks, in restaurants, or on subways—and meet surprisingly little resistance. I believe I talked to them at a time when many painful memories had become buoyant memorabilia of an almost exotic period, coupled with an awareness of their impending death. Nobody requested detailed information about why I was asking questions—it was enough for them that they could talk.

On the one hand, they were quite open and chatty, happy to straighten out what they considered to be unfair, warped visions of Nazi Germany. Sometimes they were even moved to tears by memories which they, admittedly, hadn't allowed to surface in twenty or thirty years and which seemed to ease their conscience a bit. On the other hand, without actually saying so they implied "hands off," claiming the past as their private property, and they clung to it because it was also their proof of existence. Not for a moment did they let these twelve crucial years out of their custody. These years were too precious, too many sacrifices had been made, too much pain had been inflicted to allow a younger person to just walk in and make off with their dearest possessions. They had a well-developed sense of historical turf. We are all experts at something. I was entitled to know and judge pop culture and the subculture, hippies, drugs, and rock 'n' roll, but please, let us keep our specialty, the Third Reich, they seemed to say.

A former U-boat captain turned hostile after we spent several hours talking in his posh house in an elegant suburb. To teach me a lesson about the deceptive face of evil, he mentioned with aplomb that I didn't look so radically different from a concentration camp guard, a comparison I protested vehemently. Later he called and forbade me to use his interview. He was an exception. I was warned, too—for my own good—because serious doubts about my competence began to trouble some of the old men. A seventy-eight-year-old Social Democrat and newspaperman who had had many run-ins with the Nazis stopped his talk midway and gave me a worried look and some frank advice: "What you are doing can be very harmful if it isn't done by an expert. An archaeologist, too, must know how to put the pieces together so as to reconstruct a vase."

But I wasn't trying to reconstruct a vase so much as simply trying to identify the shards of my shattered past. I was seeking neither a comprehensive sociological survey nor a single answer to the terrible conundrum that lies at the heart of Germany's history. I wanted to attempt something far more modest. I wanted to write a personal memoir, a series of ruminations that circle around questions that continue to cry out for answers. I have talked to several dozen men and women whose lives struck me as representative. I have interwoven their comments with those of my own mother and father, and this peculiar book is the result. I wanted to give expression to an anger that refuses to fade away. I wanted to come to terms with my past.

I found that the best way to do this was to write my book in English. German is a complicated, rich, and precise language. I speak German perfectly, of course: it's my native tongue. But I needed a protective wall, some distance between myself and a subject still painful and ubiquitous enough to cast a pall over my life. I wanted to separate myself from the official language of Auschwitz and so I sought an escape in the safe and beautiful world of English. Writing in another language forced me to search for linguistic images that would give my often troublesome recollections force and poignancy. I made a deal: I would sacrifice the kind of precise prose that is the birthright of a writer's native tongue, in exchange for an edgy intensity and a primitive richness that result from the very awkwardness of a second language. Writing in English was also symbolically important for me. It was the continuation of a journey that started after I decided to leave Germany. This book would never have been written if I hadn't ended up in America. Only in this country was I able to risk a look back at my homeland.

*New York City*
*June 1988*

# 1

## Herr Hitler Did That, Sweetheart

"Mommy?" I pulled on the sleeve of my mother's red gabardine coat, the one she got from America—broad-shouldered and with big gold buttons—and asked in a loud, clear voice, "Mommy, why does the man over there have only one leg?" All of a sudden she began walking faster, pulling a little on my hand, while I turned my head around and kept looking at this stranger on crutches. When we were far enough from him she said, "He lost it in the war, sweetie."

There it was again: the loss and the war. These two words were thrown at me all the time. Whatever I wanted to know about this interestingly squalid, bizarre world and the people moving around in it, these two words were always part of the answers.

Once I asked, "What is war, Mommy?"

"Mm," she sighed, and hesitated. "That's when bombs fall from the sky on people's houses, then they get hurt and everything is destroyed."

"And what are bombs?"

My mother was a beautiful woman, spontaneous, warm, and playful, but she was not interested in rational explanations or political discussions. And so she smiled her irresistible, slightly mischievous smile, her fire-red lips framing slightly crooked teeth—and the bombs in my question dropped out of my mind. Mothers have their own way of avoiding a simple answer to a four-year-old's complicated question by changing the subject to more enthralling prospects. "How about if we go home and you draw a picture with your new American crayons, the ones that smell so funny?" she suggested, and that was better than solving the mystery of the man with one leg.

The sense of loss. And of defeat. Loss of honor, loss of trust, loss of joy, and loss of many, many arms and legs. Broken heads, broken hearts, smashed bones, and visible scars filled my Germany in 1950. The era of the cripple had begun. He always seemed to sit on benches or stand on street corners, leaning firmly against the remains of a brick wall that was perhaps once a perfectly nice home, his wooden, triangular crutches resting alongside him. He wore a double-breasted, pin-striped suit, either maroon or navy blue, and smoked a cigarette with unappeasable greed. The suit was always two sizes too big—perhaps its wearer had been a fat man once, or perhaps a kindly widow had given him her deceased husband's suit as a present. One leg of the trousers, now an empty, flat piece of worsted, was neatly flipped over and fastened with two safety pins. Other times I would see the man with one arm, his sleeve tucked into his pocket. I was so glad that my daddy was in one piece. Funny, mothers were never on crutches.

Sometimes it was different. An acquaintance of my father's had a stiff, dark brown leather hand with skinny

fingers sticking out of his right sleeve, and I was afraid to
shake it when I had to greet him. Luckily, he gave us all
his real hand to shake. Another colleague had something
even more fascinating: a glass eye. "I know which one it
is," I whispered into my father's ear, but he only gave me
a little push and said, "Go and play outside."

I felt strangely drawn to these mystery men on the street.
They had an aura of quiet tragedy. They seemed to be
outcasts, and yet they belonged to my four-block territory
as much as the pale yellow Labrador dog from the hardware
store I fed my school lunches to or the chickens that lived
at the end of my street behind a brick fence topped with
prickly shrubs. These men were pale and unhealthy-
looking, with haggard features and beady eyes full of contempt, hopeless eyes that sometimes just stared into space,
at other times darted back and forth aimlessly. The men
never did anything in particular. They were just there.
Once in a while a cripple—that's what the grown-ups called
them—sat on the bench next to the communal sandbox in
the large backyard playground. Not for long, however:
there was always a mother who shouted from a window,
"Get out of here, go somewhere else, this playground is for
children!" They usually got up and left.

Children were precious in postwar Germany. Their parents wanted to protect them from the lowlifes—the beggars
and peddlers, bums and street musicians, ragpickers and,
of course, the cripples, the silent crutch men, the jobless
rubbish of society. The unfortunate ones watched us children with their melancholy faces. I wondered whether I
should risk a smile. I knew I wasn't supposed to talk to or
come close to strangers. My sister, Sylvie, who was three
years older, was given the thankless task of supervising my
frisky ways. Less curious than I and more fearful, she was

the perfect guardian. We were both warned by our mother. But about what? What was it that made her look so protective and sound so determined? There was obviously something wrong with certain men.

"Mommy, why don't these people go to work every day like Daddy?" I wanted to know one day. That one was easy to answer. "They have no work. Sometimes they can't work because they are ill, maybe some like to sit around. They have no home, I guess."

No home! Why not? I had one. "Many people were bombed out in the war," she explained. The war, always the war. I didn't understand. My father was handsome, clean-shaven, and nicely dressed, not like some of these grubby-looking men with bad teeth, dirty fingernails, and long, torn salt-and-pepper tweed coats. He wasn't on crutches nor did he knock on doors asking for food or money like the tweed-coat men did. He came home from his job at the radio station at five-thirty, and my heart beat faster when he raced around the corner on his huge black BMW motorcycle and parked it in the wooden shack he had built in the backyard next to our first-floor apartment. "Yoo-hoo," Sylvie and I would scream, hanging on to his arms and neck. We were two proud little girls when we accompanied him through the back door and into the open arms of my mother: a normal, happy German family.

Our two-and-a-half-room apartment was small, but so was I. The death of both of my great-grandparents, in 1946, together with my father's considerable finesse in dealing with Allied bureaucracy, made it possible for our family of four to have a place of our own. After living for almost three years as a daughter-in-law in my grandparents' house, my mother was happiest of all. Apartments in those days were as much in demand as cigarettes, nylons, and coffee.

Our building was a four-story, red brick prewar housing project in a predominantly working-class neighborhood in the suburbs of Hamburg. It had balconies overlooking the backyard. I liked the place but my mother always complained about wanting to live in the city, in an elegant villa. We had one living room, one bedroom, a small kitchen, a bathroom with a tub, and a small room which my sister and I shared. There were no passionate discussions about wallpaper, furniture, refrigerators, or other luxury items because none were available. We had kept the bulky, dark furniture of my great-grandparents, but my mother managed to add some style and color, and transformed our room into a pink kingdom by painting parrots and children with balloons on the walls.

In 1945 everybody in Germany started out on an equal footing. The uniformity of the Nazi years gave way to the uniformity of a common emotional experience, and for a short time Germany resembled a classless society in which poverty was a mass movement. Nobody cared whether Herr Meier from next door owned a factory "before the war," or that he had driven a big Mercedes and lived in a villa with servants. Now he rode a bike to work like almost everyone else, and his wife hung up the laundry in the backyard like all the other wives and widows. This involuntary socialism began to fade around 1950. The class system slowly crept back and with it came an intolerance for those who failed to participate wholeheartedly in the country's rapid economic recovery.

People didn't want to know about those who had seen too much and couldn't forget. If you couldn't do away with the rubble and the memories of war, you were on your way to becoming one of the unlucky pariahs. Backs began to turn and doors began to shut at the sight of begging eyes and ragged clothes. But these citizens couldn't be sent away. The concentration camps were gone. They stayed right there, giving postwar street life a sense of realism, poignancy, and truth. The master race outmastered itself. Germany was still in rags.

My sister and I played on the streets most of the time because that's where our mother sent us (we had never heard of kindergarten). Once a week, a little old man in a long, dark coat and fingerless wool gloves trotted down the cobblestone street on which I lived, holding a violin case under his arm. He went directly to the backyard and stood in the middle of it. We kids followed him at a respectable distance and watched him take the violin out of a case lined with faded and torn royal-blue velvet. What a peculiar instrument it was: piercing, sad, and a touch dissonant, not like the soft, swinging sounds of Ted Heath's orchestra my mother often listened to on the BBC. When he started to play, his gaze wandered up and down the windows, and after a few minutes of music wafting into the quiet suburban sky, several windows began shutting with an angry slam. I could see some silhouettes behind the white transparent curtains—just standing there, motionless. Sometimes the curtains were carefully pulled aside just a crack, and there was a brief, suspicious glance from an old face or just a curious, stretched neck. Nobody stood openly at the window and enjoyed the music. (Germans do not customarily grant itinerant musicians unauthorized auditions.)

He usually stopped after about ten minutes, and then, finally, some windows opened and the more charitable souls threw tiny, hard packages at him. He eagerly collected the brown crumbled wrapping paper containing the five-, ten-, and twenty-pfennig coins, and put the money in his pocket, packed up the fiddle, and bowed politely toward the windows with the shadows behind the curtains. As he left, smiling, I felt something like envy. I wished that I was the kind of person people showered with pfennigs, so I could buy sweets.

I was shy, but also inquisitive, and nothing could keep me away from the characters who wandered in and out of my street—not even my mother's warning "not to get too close to strangers." There were beggars who were occasionally fed with big liverwurst sandwiches or bowls of soup, and once my mother had a fit when she saw me sitting side by side with one, slurping homemade bouillon with one spoon between us.

Once a week, on Saturdays, my sister and I received twenty-five pfennigs straight out of the pocket of my father's tweed sports coat. A fortune. I ran immediately to Moeller's delicatessen around the corner and purchased the only thing worth my money: a small, gray, rectangular paper box without any labels. We called it the "American wonder box" because it came from U.S. Army surplus, and the chewing-gum balls and candies it contained would usually make my day.

Whenever my mother got together for coffee with Tante Reiniger, our feisty next-door neighbor—which happened about once a day—the conversation turned inevitably to food. They compared everything: real coffee versus ersatz coffee, butter versus margarine, jam made out of real fruit versus artificial honey or sugar-beet syrup. Whenever Tante Reiniger sent me out to buy an eighth of a pound of real coffee her face was always proud and full of anticipation. Sometimes she would say, "Binchen, *Schatz*, could you get me three cigarettes, you know the brand, Supra, okay?" and give me twenty pfennigs, which meant that the remaining five pfennigs were for me.

Money was important to me. My parents talked about money all the time, with tense faces. In their opinion, there were two categories of people: those with money and those without it. You could tell by whether they had a car or not. My father wanted one. Sometimes, when my father was angry, he said that my mother "threw money out the window," and that she was a person "obsessed with luxury."

I thought she spent too much time forcing unrequested food upon innocent children. I'll bet there weren't any German children in the early fifties who were allowed to leave even the tiniest piece of liver on their plates. I hated the look and smell of fat meat, and my sister hated the raisins that were hidden in the semolina pudding. But my mother pressed the food on us even when we started gagging, and not without pointing out our thanklessness and the thousands of Germans who would be happy just to sniff a piece of meat with lots of fat on it. On the other hand, I loved potatoes, cabbage, and turnips, much to the surprise of my parents, who felt that these were only for poor people, or "proles," as my father called them. "We had enough of that stuff during the war," they both said.

"Your mother speaks funny," said Helga Schramm one day. "She's a foreigner," I answered with a feeling of superiority. (I liked the German word *Ausländerin* because it sounded so exotic.) "She's from Lithuania." That explained a lot. Not that I had the faintest idea where Lithuania was, but I was sure it had something to do with the fact that my mother looked like nobody else. She was colorful, elegant, and proud, with a small waist and an impressive bust. Her beautiful face had classic features and a flawless complexion, and her dark-blond hair with a platinum streak was piled up in a twist or gathered in a bun covered with a fancy black net. Sometimes she tried to smuggle tiny bangs onto her forehead, but my father pushed them back with saliva and determination, saying, "Please, no shopgirl's hairdo." She obeyed with a sigh.

When we walked down the street together, heads turned and whistles were heard. I didn't understand why women looked at her so disdainfully while men smacked their lips. But I did know why she didn't wear navy-blue tailored men's suits, knitted cardigans with mended elbows, high-buttoned blouses, stockings with runs in them, and shoes with worn-off heels like most of the other women I saw. We got packages from America.

Often, when the doorbell rang my sister and I rushed to the door, although we weren't allowed to open it. We were hoping for the mailman, a most popular man dressed in blue, because there was a chance that he would hand my mother a little yellow slip and utter the sentence that sent us spinning into uncontrollable exaltation: "Frau Reichel, you have a package from America!"

For the rest of the day our thoughts would be on the magic box from overseas, and the next day we would go to the main post office and pick it up from customs. Of course, we wanted our mother to open it right away. If it was near Christmas, no such luck; if it was the middle of the year, she allowed us to watch her unpack. We would actually shiver with excitement. Who would have guessed that these shabby-looking packages were bursting with colors, smells, shapes, and consistencies I hadn't even known existed. They came from my mother's Lithuanian relatives, and I loved them dearly even though I had never met them.

"This is for me"—our mother put the blue Maxwell House tin can aside—"and this too"—and she placed three copies of *The Saturday Evening Post* next to the coffee. She loved the covers, many of which were painted by Norman

Rockwell, her favorite. All three of us sat on the floor and watched one delight after another emerge from the package. There were chocolate bars and "kisses"—little pointed things wrapped in silver foil. They tasted so much better than German chocolate. The best were the round, colored candies called M&M's, but since everything had to be divided in two, I wondered whether my mother, who lacked a certain Germanic correctness, could be trusted to count so many M&M's. The children in the neighborhood envied our foreign treasures, but I couldn't bring myself to share even one piece of American chocolate.

The sweets were only part of the treats. Aunt Barbara in America must have known that German children were not snappy dressers in those days. Why else would she have sent us two breathtakingly beautiful, flower-patterned chenille bathrobes in yellow and turquoise? But the unforgettable moment came when my mother unwrapped a pair of shocking-pink furry slippers in the shape of rabbits. "For me!" I instantly cried, and was happy for the first time that I had smaller feet than my sister, because the slippers turned out to be my size. I would have loved to wear them on the street! At the bottom of the package were two coloring books, one called "Alice in Wonderland" and the other one called "Mickey Mouse." We were in heaven. What a country, this America.

"They are pretty rich there and have everything," my mother said, adding wistfully, "My father always wanted me to go to America and not to Germany." She should have been happy because she always got the biggest share: shoes in all colors and shapes, fabric, seamed nylons with fancy heels, gloves, scarves, sunglasses, lipsticks, compacts, and many buttons. The only one who didn't benefit directly from our American connection was my father. Except for an occasional plaid wool shirt, there was nothing of interest for him in the packages. He didn't mind, he wanted the three of us to look spectacular; our limelight would reflect well on him and gain him the attention he liked.

We often took the streetcar into the city to go shopping. My sister and I knew the site of the ruins inside and out— we sometimes played hide-and-seek in them, which was fun.

"Mommy, who made all that *kaputt*?" asked Sylvie, who pressed her nose against the window until it fogged up.

"Herr Hitler did that, sweetheart," said Mommy matter-of-factly, and Sylvie and I both nodded as if we understood completely.

"But why?" I asked.

"He was crazy and mean and that's why he started the war," she said, tapping her foot impatiently. She often wore my favorite shoes, open toes, platform high heels with ankle straps in bright red, which looked perfect on her shapely legs, which she exhibited as generously as her décolletage. Her summer dress was a cotton print with little houses on it and had a narrow waist that was accentuated by a wide red leather belt with gold studs. Her ears were half covered with big white plastic earrings, the kind children always want to grab. I thought she looked like a fairy-tale princess and I wanted to look exactly like her when I grew up.

My mother was thirty years old in 1950, and when other kids asked me what her profession was, I said, "*Hausfrau*," not without satisfaction, because it meant that she was home all day. Most mothers were *Hausfrauen* but many were also widows, like my friend Renate's mother.

"I lost my father in the war," Renate told me, and I wondered how that was possible. Renate's mother worked and so did my other friend Gabi's mother, although her

father was still alive. My father would never have allowed
my mother to work every day. "What would people say?"
he would ask. "That I can't make enough money to support
my family?" I felt sorry for the girls and for their mothers,
who couldn't sit around all morning and afternoon and drink
coffee like my mom and Tante Reiniger.

But there was also an element of envy. Gabi, Renate,
and Annegret, another friend, had something I didn't have:
a key around their necks, a symbol of mastery and independence tied to a piece of brown string. They could do
what they wanted, eat when they were hungry, listen to
the radio, and go in and out as often as they pleased. They
could investigate interesting-looking books and mysterious
drawers. My parents didn't want me to be friends with
these "latchkey kids." "These are poor people's children,"
my father said. They were creatures with a flaw. Working
moms are bad, I concluded.

Sometimes I felt lonely. The street was quiet, the older
children were in school, and everybody else seemed to have
disappeared. It wasn't fun to play with dolls all by myself.
I had to stay within my mother's reach, but I occasionally
managed to sneak away to the backyard around the corner
and get a good look at the fascinating people who lived
there. There were many girls my age with pretty, colorful
long skirts and at least as many boys with dirty faces and
big black eyes. They all had black hair and dark skin, and
the women wore scarves around their heads and golden
rings in their ears. Most of the men had gold teeth and wore
diamond rings on their pinkies. They sat inside the house
and played cards in the middle of the afternoon.

When they saw me for the first time, they laughed and
waved at me to come closer. They were friendly and stroked
my hair and felt it between their fingers. That made me

uneasy, but I let them do it because I thought they were
magical people and that maybe some of that magic would
rub off on me. They were called Gypsies, and people said
they stole and had lice. My mother didn't want me to play
with them. I had to be careful on my excursions to the
"dangerous zone" because we had the kind of neighbors
who would have asked immediately, "Frau Reichel, I saw
your daughter with the Gypsies, does she have your permission?" The neighbors always watched each other and
special attention was given to us children. We had no
privacy.

Another unauthorized playmate was Dagmar, who lived
on the same block. My parents shook their heads over my
attachment to her. She wasn't my mother's idea of a pretty
girl, with her thick glasses plastered with tape, to adjust
her eyesight. Dagmar also had something that was absolutely forbidden to me. She had pierced ears and tiny coral
heart earrings. Absolutely beautiful. My mother visibly
shuddered when I suggested wearing what I considered a
daring and yet chic combination I had seen on Dagmar:
dark blue sweatpants worn under a dress on cold winter
days.

Clothes were extremely important and Dagmar's ward-
robe was an unfailing tip-off for my parents. Apparently,
there was a difference between her little red felt hat with
the elastic band under her chin, which she wore on Sun-
days, and my homemade crisp seersucker dress with puffed
sleeves that tied in the back with a big bow. Dagmar's father
came home from work on a bike, and on warm summer
evenings he would sit on the stoop in front of the house
clad in undershirt and suspenders, guzzling beer out of a
bottle. He had been a soldier in the war and was now a
factory worker, and for that reason Dagmar wasn't a suitable

playmate for me, my father said. I didn't understand why, but I knew I didn't agree and I kept playing with her just the same, choosing locations that were not directly in front of my mother's nose.

In addition to pierced ears, cabbage, cripples, poverty, Gypsies, and latchkey kids, there was another group of people whose credibility was questionable because of something my father had a strange name for. When he saw me trading scooters with Hartmut Kiesinger one day, his face turned grave. Later, inside the house, he told me, "I don't want you to play with the Kiesinger kids. The parents are Nazis." Interesting word, but what did it mean?

I knew that it was somehow related to those other powerful words: war, loss, bombs, hunger. Not to mention the name that came up often, that certain Herr Hitler. He was the one who caused the war, the bombs, the cripples, and all the other bad things. What a mighty person he must have been. Almost like God.

"Dad, can we see the stamps?" we asked whenever we saw our father sitting at his old-fashioned rolltop desk writing letters or paying bills. "Oh, come on, kids, not again," he'd moan. In a special drawer at the bottom he kept three sheets of stamps in brown, green, and burgundy depicting that man he called "a criminal," shown in profile and looking like other normal older men on the street. "They'll be very special one day," he always explained as he carefully took out the stamps. We would stand there with rapt attention, hands behind our backs, and gaze at the evil from the drawer, until Daddy put Herr Hitler back into the file.

My friend Renate and I had a variety of games and diversions. One day we were playing hopscotch when something strange happened. Hans-Jürgen and Dieter, the two oldest Hoffmann sons, were standing not too far from us, laughing and gesticulating with their arms. While Dieter leaned against the wall holding his stomach to control his laughter, Hans-Jürgen stood there in a funny stiff posture, one arm raised while the other pressed a little black comb onto his upper lip. Renate and I watched for a few seconds, shrugged our shoulders, and went back to our hopscotch. Boys have silly ideas about games.

Suddenly we heard a shrill, angry voice. We stopped hopping around and gaped at Frau Hoffmann, who had Dieter's arm in a firm grip. "Who scrawled this on the wall?" she shouted, pointing to the side of the house. Her face was contorted and almost purple. "I was watching you from the window. Didn't I tell you to stop that nonsense?" She shook Dieter's arm a bit more. He and his brother were perhaps more embarrassed over being scolded in public than they were ashamed of what they did. But what *did* they do?

Frau Hoffmann took the boys home, and we waited until they were gone before running over to the wall to discover the reason for her explosion. We saw some words we couldn't read and a big, funny-looking cross with hooks which I had seen a few times before on walls around the neighborhood. Whatever the boys did, they deserved a spanking, Renate and I decided.

Afterward, we went to her apartment. "Oh, this looks exactly like my Uncle Kurt," I exclaimed, pointing to a photograph of a man in uniform. In my grandmother's house there was a picture of her son Kurt wearing the same kind of uniform. "That's my father. He fell in the war," said Renate with a proud little smile. How could someone "fall" in the war? I knew that it meant that he never returned. Uncle Kurt, my father's younger brother, came back from Russia and didn't "fall" in the war; he was in good health, and visited us frequently because he was a doctor and a bachelor. That's why he had so much time on his hands, said my mother. However, he was the exception that proved the rule: photographs of men in uniform on the living-room wall usually meant that the fathers were dead or "missing."

In the spring of 1950, my mother and I accompanied Sylvie to her first day in school. It was customary in Germany to give children a big, colorful paper cone filled with sweets and school supplies such as pencil boxes and erasers. "You'll get one too," my mother assured me with a confident look when she saw my longing eyes. Sylvie looked unhappy. Her button-nosed face was pale with apprehension and the enormous, freshly ironed pink bows holding her long hair, which was braided and turned up into a "monkey swing," were dangling over each ear. She wore the gray coat Mom had made her out of a military blanket, which had the extra-long hem we had on all our clothes.

"Children grow so fast," she said, and looked at Sylvie, who had long matchstick legs and not an ounce of fat on her fragile body. "She was born during the war," my mother sometimes said, embracing Sylvie suddenly and smiling at her with sparkling eyes. She did that often and I didn't like it. Why did I suddenly cease to exist? It was as though being born during the war was something special, a big advantage that gave you the affection of your mom.

It was a gloomy day when we walked down Gustav-Adolf-Strasse. On our left were two bombed-out buildings with pieces of brick walls sticking up into the smoggy sky. "Oh, these ugly ruins everywhere," my mother muttered, and furrowed her brows. On the right was the freight-train depot with cars full of coal. There were boys with zinc buckets scurrying around trying to steal coal. But there was something else that day, something I had never seen before.

On the ramp next to the tracks stood unusual green cars without tops and square boxes without wheels and windows and with long tubes in the front.

"Jeeps and tanks," said my mother when I asked what they were. There were lots of men. Some sat in the jeeps, some were peeking out from holes in the middle of the tanks, and some just stood around talking and smoking cigarettes. They all wore uniforms that matched the color of the cars, and on their heads sat berets pulled over one ear. When we came close enough to hear what they were saying, I could tell they were foreigners because I knew they were speaking English. My father sometimes said to us in English, "Good night, girls," and that had a similar sound. Why did Mom have to walk faster, pulling my arm, whenever we came across something unusual? The men looked friendly to me, even more so when broad grins lit up their young freckled faces. I grinned back.

"Come on, Binchen," my mother said, slightly annoyed. I had a feeling that she didn't want to get to know them. She ordered us never to go there and talk to these strangers. And when I told her later that I had seen boys on their bikes talking to them, she snapped, "Well, girls don't do that," and that was that.

"Who are these men in uniform?"

"Tommies," Mom said.

A few minutes later we arrived at the monumental, prisonlike red brick schoolhouse. Hundreds of children with mothers and relatives were gathered in front of the old building. Hundreds of paper cones were pressed into the children's arms. Hundreds of the same extra-long hems on coats made from uniforms and blankets, the same knitted brown wool stockings in laced-up brown shoes, the same school satchels on their backs, and many neat braids tied with big bows framing pale, insecure faces. These were the ones born in 1943 and 1944, the years of bombing raids over Germany, of sirens, collapsing buildings, frightened mothers and crying babies. These were the precious children, the comfort of the dark moments of despair, the reason for wanting to survive at any cost. These were their mothers' dearest.

Without consciously remembering it, they had seen and heard too much. They had been misplaced and disguised, carried by fleeing mothers over borders and hidden in carts. They had been lost in bombing attacks and were found alive under piles of rubble. They were the war babies—resilient survivors, but also fearful little souls with brittle smiles. Five years after the year zero, millions of such children took their first step into de-Nazified uniformity. The school opened its doors under Allied supervision.

I had counted the weeks and days that brought me closer to the long-awaited event: my first day of school. It was March 1953, and I was all set with a new satchel, a paper cone, and a short hairdo. I didn't want braids, they were old-fashioned. I wore a navy-blue coat with gold buttons and a normal hem, white socks, and brown loafers.

It was still cold, but the sun was shining. We walked the same route, to the same school—just as we had done with my sister three years before. Not much had changed. There were still ruins on one side of the street, and boys were still picking up coal. The Tommies hadn't left, but I still hadn't talked to them, although I could have said, "How do you do?" But men in uniform didn't interest me in the least on that day.

When we reached the school we could hardly believe our eyes. I had never seen so many children in my life. There were fewer pale faces and more pink, plump cheeks, and most school satchels were brand-new and not handed down by older siblings. I felt uneasy with so many people around me. I was afraid. My mom told me that a lot of children were born right after the war like me. "You are a peace baby," she said, and smiled at me with great confidence before she kissed me goodbye.

We walked into the school, were counted by the teachers, and divided into classes. I ended up with fifty-two other girls—my future classmates—squeezed into one room. Fräulein Wybkema, my teacher, introduced herself. She was tall, skinny, and had something brusque and modern about her. First, we sang a song and then we had to recite our name, date of birth, name and profession of our parents, and our home address. I was happy to announce that my mother's name was Suzana, quickly adding that she was a foreigner, that her profession was *Hausfrau*, and that my father's name was Karl-Heinz and his profession was actor, which he really wasn't anymore but I couldn't think of the name for what he actually did. We sat two to a desk and my seatmate was Jutta Gerhof. It was her turn. Mother's profession: widow and employee. Father's profession: soldier—killed at Stalingrad.

The war was far from being over.

# 2

# *How Come You Didn't
Die Laughing?*

"**B**inchen, come downstairs. I want you to see what's on TV!" my father yelled one day from the living room. I was immediately suspicious. Whenever I was asked to watch TV it was usually something my father considered an icon of popular enlightenment, such as the German-dubbed *Perry Como Show* (a particular favorite). It had nothing to do with Perry that evening, however, but with a much more animated and controversial celebrity whose audience evinced an enthusiasm that is rarely aroused on any stage by any performer. No, the show that evening in 1964 wasn't about imported American culture, but about the spellbinding dictatorship of a folk hero with a brushlike mustache.

After years of conspicuous silence, in a sudden fit of educational responsibility, German TV stations in the early sixties had finally begun attempting to shed some light on "the rise and fall of the Third Reich." These special reports were usually shown at unpopular times, squeezed in between reruns of worthy but clunky German dramas and documentaries with subjects like Harz Mountain wood-carvers.

"You've got to see this," my father said excitedly, as if he was attending the premiere of a long-awaited extravaganza, and sat down next to me. Our TV set was an atrocious piece of furniture on four stubby legs with two doors that could be locked. "Mom, you wanna watch too?" I called from the living room. "Oh no, that's too much for me. I don't need to see that again," she moaned, and disappeared into the kitchen.

Of course, by the time I was seventeen I had some idea of what the Third Reich looked like. There had been snippets here and there on TV and in magazines for as long as I could remember. Still, when I saw those images as part of a continuous and coherent narrative, the concentrated horror sent shivers down my spine and my arms had goose bumps all over. I loved these documentaries and could never get enough of them. They were fantastic, hallucinatory, and often hysterically funny. I was both fascinated and repelled: something about these surreal, almost slapstick choreographed marches kept me mesmerized, as they did my parents' generation thirty years ago. The only difference was that I simply couldn't grasp it. It was beyond me. I stared in disbelief at the mock opera unfolding in front of me on the television screen, thinking, "This wasn't for real. It had to be a joke." What I saw couldn't seriously have existed. How come the entire German nation didn't die laughing? And if even I sensed that an entire people marching around in military uniform was bound to end in disaster, how come so few people realized it at the time?

But the storm troopers with their silly caps strapped under their square chins and a nasty little smirk on their lips were nothing compared to the ridiculous nincompoop wrapped in brown poplin. Why wasn't he booed away from the microphone when he spewed his nonsense at the people with his shrill voice, strange dialect, and funny diction? This character with a thin, dyspeptic mouth, a greasy fringe over his forehead, and a theater prop for a mustache was obviously a creepy lunatic—the very picture of a coarse, pathetic, and pompous megalomaniac. Why didn't everybody say to one another, "Let's go home, this is too outlandish"?

"Jesus, were you all blind?" I blurted out with a look at my father. "You don't understand," he replied. "It was a different time, people saw things differently. It's not comprehensible today." We could never argue this point. Supposedly, we young people couldn't understand—and perhaps weren't supposed to—how such an insane man could gain such power, run amok, and get away with it. Yet what was the difference whether a guy talked dangerous rubbish in 1934 or in 1964?

When I saw this cretin stretch his arm in an inane gesture to ecstatic applause, or pat a German shepherd's ears and children's blond locks to the gapes of infatuated women, I questioned the sanity of the entire German people. They should have had their collective head examined. What a strange world my parents had lived in . . . I couldn't picture them in this silly environment.

Did people actually *live* like that? Everything was organized, from the first cry in the cradle to the last breath on the battlefield. Everybody's life belonged to the Führer. "Without you, we are nothing," went one slogan. Mothers who had more than four children were rewarded with an Iron Cross. (My Aunt Trude, my father's younger sister, had a close brush with that decoration—she had three children between 1938 and 1943.) It was as though Hitler was the nation's sweetheart, a cult figure, beloved and cherished. The most puzzling part was that he was considered a "ladies' man." There were allusions in my family, tinged with irony, to the fact that my grandmother belonged to that undeterred group of women of all ages who saw Hitler as a charming devil with a godlike character. (I should have asked her about it, but we never talked about such subjects in her house.) I wondered where Herr Hitler hid the notorious charm he was said to display in "social situations." After all, when he was angry he bit into the carpets, I had heard.

Eva Braun, his girlfriend, followed him like a puppy, always two steps behind as if his precious aura emanated blinding rays. Why did she have to wear puffed sleeves, a natty hunter's hat, or an apron? My father had told me that before Eva, Hitler had an affair with his niece, Geli, who killed herself because of him. It seemed as if German women in the Third Reich were gratified to have a high-ranking politician confirm them in their boring role as *Hausfrauen* and mothers. *Ach*, that Adolf, in spite of his cantankerous behavior he was just a big boy at heart, a little obstinate and pigheaded maybe, but that could be forgiven. The man before him was Hindenburg, a senile, stiff old fart with antiquated ideas. Hitler was a kid, a dizzy dictator, with his hair hanging over his eye and that distorted shy grin. Perhaps they wanted to mother him a bit.

Watching the footage, I could see how quickly National Socialism had moved to purge the *Kultur* of un-German elements. As early as 1933 the Nazis were staging book burnings in the streets. The people seemed to be thrilled. "We consign to the flames the writings of Thomas Mann, Franz Kafka, Sigmund Freud, Stefan Zweig," some Brownshirts and upright, helpful citizens were shouting. When I looked around our living room I saw none of these books on the shelves, and I knew they hadn't been burned. My father wasn't the kind of man who would be interested in Freud's psychological discoveries, let alone be caught brooding over the dark world of Kafka. (We had just read Kafka in school, and I loved him.)

But even worse than their acts of destruction was what the Nazis created, especially their movies: all those worthy citizens with determined chins riding, flying, and kissing for Germany. I was cringing in my chair. I could imagine nothing more repulsive than precocious, regimented Hitler Youth members blabbering about blood honor instead of minding their own business and listening to the Beatles and watching *Bonanza* like normal kids.

"Did you actually watch this retarded stuff?" I asked my father. "God, no," he answered, amused but also slightly annoyed. "I loved American movies. Myrna Loy, Dorothy Lamour . . . but there were fine German actors too." I frowned and thought, "Sure, but who got Marlene Dietrich?"

Everything was *verboten* in Nazi Germany, including all "foreign elements," and especially "nigger music" and "decadent art." The Nazis confiscated thousands of paintings and showed them later in Munich in a special exhibition to warn the public. It drew the biggest crowd ever and Hitler had the show closed immediately. "Who's decadent here? Look at the Nazis!" I howled, practically writhing in my chair. This drew a strange look from my father. I always suspected that the fine arts, particularly the German Expressionists, remained a total mystery to him. I think the colors were too loud for him, and the forms too disorderly. When they showed the monumental sculptures of Arno

Breker—not exactly a Picasso—and oversized portraits of the Führer in medieval armor, I gasped, "Boy, no wonder all the great thinkers and artists immediately fled the country. Didn't you feel you were being made fun of with this *Kultur Kitsch?*" "No, we didn't take that too seriously," said my father, shaking his head.

What bothered me most were the constant, ugly attacks on the Jews. One event in particular struck me: *Kristallnacht,* in 1938, a pretty name for a very ugly night. The television program showed Jewish stores all over the country, from small shops to big, elegant emporiums, but what a sight they were! As if a hurricane had swept over them. Windows were broken, doors smashed in—one could almost hear the shattering sound of breaking glass—and smeared on the remaining jagged shards and on the walls was the word *Jude.* As if that wasn't enough, there were viciously grinning Brownshirts in front of the stores guarding the doors, legs wide apart, hands behind their backs, gleefully keeping customers out. Curious bystanders gaped at the spectacle, shrugged their shoulders, and walked away.

I didn't see any protest. The Germans were cowards, that's what they were! I felt like screaming at so much injustice. This ostentatious, brutal raid couldn't have been a big secret, could it? I had always identified with minorities, at school, on the street, and I could imagine the shock of arriving one day at the store where your friends and neighbors had shopped for twenty years and finding everything destroyed. Yet the destruction itself wasn't nearly as bad as the fact that it took place out in the open, before everybody's eyes, and without resistance. What a betrayal! The Jews must certainly have lost all illusions about loyalty and friendship on that day.

I tried to imagine how it would feel to go to school one

morning and find all the Greek snack bars and Italian piz-
zerias vandalized. What would my mother say if a group
of policemen knocked at our door and confiscated all her
elegant clothes and forbade her to see American movies
because she was Lithuanian? Or what if my father were
told that he couldn't get a certain job because he was German? Would they take it? What was the matter with the
Germans? Why did they always have to destroy everything
around them, and start wars over and over again?

After one full hour of militaristic hoopla and enough
swastika flags to wrap the whole continent, the mood projected from the TV screen into our living room gradually
became more solemn. The slight touch of satire faded as
more and more jackboots marched into foreign countries
with master-race smiles. The Third Reich was beginning
to make me nervous, and my high-pitched laughter and
giggling over the nutty dictator and his equally nutty *Volk*
slowly subsided. Hundreds of thousands of Wehrmacht
soldiers smiled bravely on the road to Russia. Houses flew
through the air while field hospitals filled up with limbs
shot to pieces and covered with blood-drenched bandages.

I looked away for a few seconds.

"Stalingrad," said Daddy.

I saw a white, icy world populated with stiff, frozen
bodies by the roadside, rags wrapped around hands, feet,
and ears, icicles hanging from beards and noses. Nature
can't be fooled by subhuman theories: Red Army or Brown
Army—they were all equal in the snow.

"*Ach*, Hitler was already over the edge. Everybody knew
that the war was lost after Stalingrad," said my father, who
was spared the Russian battle.

That wasn't the end of the destruction, however, and I
was beginning to get weary. Next the German sky was

covered with American and British airplanes, and bombs were falling from the sky like toys, sounding like firecrackers on New Year's Eve. "Hearing that whistling sound makes me shiver," said my mother, who had dropped in to put some Cheez Doodles on the coffee table, while she absent-mindedly dried her hands on her apron. She could under-stand something she could identify with—the war in front of her own door in 1943–44, in Berlin and Hamburg. "Never in my life will I forget those sounds," she said.

As children, we had asked her over and over again to tell us how everybody had to pack their belongings several times a night and sit, petrified with fear, in the shelters until the bombing raids were over. She said that people never un-packed their stuff, it stood by the door, ready to be picked up at the sound of the warning sirens. This is probably why she's such a neatnik as well as being the best suitcase packer I've ever seen.

Germany was in bad shape by this time. There weren't many soldiers left; mostly women, young and old, with crying children in their arms or clinging to their hands. They ran down the streets in a frenzy while buildings col-lapsed, pushing carts piled high with boxes and furniture, overstuffed suitcases tied shut with ropes. Evacuation time. That wasn't how people looked who have illusions and want to win wars, but I really didn't feel sorry for them; it was their own fault.

"We lived in terror," sighed my mother. My father didn't say anything. He looked exhausted.

"All done by the Tommies and Amis!" Mom added re-proachfully, but as she spoke another image appeared on the screen and her expression changed. It looked like a home movie, without any sound, which made it more portentous. Naked men and women—despite the poor quality of the

film we could see their surprised and shameful expressions—were herded to the edge of a large trench by men
in riding pants, and made to kneel down, hands behind
their heads, before slumping and falling over in silence.

"I can't watch this!" My mother almost gagged and ran
out while my father and I remained in our chairs, silent. I
felt sick, but something unfathomable made me stare at
those dark, grainy black-and-white images. Who had the
heart to film all that? Next we saw people lined up in long
rows wearing big stars on their coats and jackets, among
them children with teddy bears. A random blow with a
switch on someone's back accompanied by a vicious grin.
Every time I see SS men together with Jews I see smirks,
sneers, and cackles of delight. That disturbs me more than
anything else. "I only did my duty," they would whine
later. Really? Does one smile while torturing human beings?
Was it one's duty to enjoy killing? I feel nothing but an
overwhelming sense of hatred when I see those grinning
faces—German faces.

Concentration camps. Ovens and smoke. The barracks,
the barbed wire, and all those sad-eyed creatures in striped
clothes. Among them, in a relaxed, affable mood, small
groups of SS men were standing together, slightly bored—
continuous killing is apparently monotonous. They chatted
with each other, rocking up and down on the balls of their
feet, clad in meticulously shined boots, giving a vigilant
Rolf a pat on his head—they're so fond of animals—and
laughing heartily.

The next image to flicker on the screen was of D-day
with its deadly logic of punishment and revenge. The end
of the Third Reich came fast and furious, with more battles
and bombs and so many different uniforms that I lost track
of who was who. The ones with the pot helmets were the

Americans, with their broad, reckless smiles and fetching sunglasses. Finally, they ran footage of the war criminals at the Nuremberg trials. What a group! They looked arrogant and somewhat irritated by the accusations against them, as though they had nothing to feel guilty about. It reminded me of the Eichmann trial, which had taken place only a couple of years before. I remember it only because my father was furious that this sensational case wasn't being used as a contemporary history lesson in my school; it wasn't even mentioned. Eichmann was a gaunt, surly man with thinning hair and a bored face I found weird and alienating—the man was too average. There was nothing devilish or sensational about him, so why should I be interested? I wasn't so keen on people his age anyway. They all looked the same to me.

After so many frames of a world I had no connection with, I grew impatient with the documentary. The spell was broken now that the fantastic, destructive Third Reich had fallen, taking with it the exotic and the bizarre. The rest of it I knew myself: how old Adenauer became the first chancellor and we had a *Wirtschaftswunder*, which meant that everybody could now buy Volkswagens and kidney-shaped tables.

My father turned off the television and there was silence in the living room. The happy, fresh face of the new *Bundesrepublik* made us yawn. I didn't feel like talking and immediately got up, thinking, "You all can keep your Führer and his insane terror. I've got nothing to do with your wars," and left. Nobody was holding me back. The documentary had initially seemed like a promising and entertaining thriller, but the ending had come as a shock. This was no movie; I couldn't go home laughing, shaking it all off. The

Third Reich actually happened. I was stuck with that bitter truth.

Back in my room I felt safe again, and took a deep breath, relieved at having escaped the Nazi ghosts in the living room. Surrounded by my own personally selected and approved idols and objects of interest and infatuation, I began to think. What I had just seen was so horrible that it screamed for explanations. I tried to think of a reason—any reason—but I couldn't find any. Seeing all the atrocities the Nazis had committed was different from just vaguely knowing about them. The contempt for the past and the old Germans was ignited again, but there was also an injection of energy, a will and a wish: never again.

I was scared too. All the uniforms, the bombs, the war, the concentration camps looked so dangerous, and it all happened only nineteen years ago. Didn't terrible sins get punished one day? What if someone decided to kill all Germans?

I was glad that my father didn't involve me in further discussions. How could so much evil have existed, and why were the Germans the inventors and perpetrators of it? There was something wrong with the whole Nazi phenomenon; it didn't fit together. What did it mean when people said, "We had no idea," as they always did? I had just seen a documentary about real events, actions that happened right under their noses: burned books, *Kristallnacht*, people lined up on the streets—that must have been pretty hard to ignore. Yet all the adults ever said about it was: "You can't possibly understand."

# 3

# What Did You Do
# in the War, Daddy?

My father was not so much a Nazi as he was a nar-
cissist—and I don't know whether that was better for
my relationship with him. Both conditions share similar
characteristics, such as vanity, selfishness, and grandiosity.
That he ended up hating the Nazis is to his credit and must
be attributed to his innate sense of right and wrong, his
revulsion toward violence, and his ability to judge morally
and take sides. He was more clever than intelligent, and his
reactions were those of a man with a conscience, not a
brilliant mind. That he was mutinous and contrary by nature also helped. I saw flashes of these virtues when I was
a little girl, but their spark grew dimmer as I grew older,
and I don't know whether the change was due to my eyes
or his heart, or both. He slowly became inaccessible, priggish, intolerant, and disinterested. At some point, I began
to feel that his shortcomings went beyond his own individual character.

Why are German fathers such a problem? What is wrong

with them? Not all fathers, of course, but the ones born between 1900 and 1925, all of whom are former citizens of Nazi Germany, regardless of whether they were fervent supporters, passive participants, or declared enemies of the Third Reich. It is their fate to be linked to a reprehensible crime that was carried out in their name, and they will never rise above suspicion as long as they live. It is a past they can't shake off; and neither can their children. To be a daughter of a father who was twenty-one years old in 1933 always felt to me like having a dark secret, a weak spot, like the Germanic folk hero Siegfried, who killed an eight-headed dragon and then bathed in the creature's blood to make himself invulnerable, without noticing the oak leaf that had fallen on his back. I would often feel a sharp, poignant spear of pain through that spot: shame.

"It must be the war that did something to them," was the conclusion my teenage friends and I always came up with whenever we complained about our strict and distant fathers, judging them by instinct rather than knowledge. And I really don't know what my father would have been like without the war, or how much it changed him for better or worse. Exactly how did those nightmarish years affect someone like my father, who detested the Nazis but also grew up among them? By the time he was seventy he had become a cynical and callous man without wisdom to spare and without great expectations for the future.

Nineteen eighty-two was the year I began to think about my father in a new way. By that time we were living in two different worlds. I was in New York, where I'd moved in 1975 as a struggling journalist, and he was in Majorca, Spain, where he'd moved in 1965 as a carefree pensioner after a successful career as an advertising director and pop-music lyricist. I lived in perpetual conflict with him, a sit-

uation that hasn't changed much to this day. My refusal to
play the part of a perfectly pliant daughter for too long
usually reduced us to two actors who performed on separate
stages and made our sporadic meetings joyless and often
hostile events. This time, however, my freshly liberated
curiosity transformed him. He wasn't merely my obstrep-
erous old father whom I thought I had extricated myself
from forever, but a precious—and all too mortal—witness
to the Nazi era who needed to be interrogated.

Convinced that investigations of the human condition
should start at home, I went to Majorca and asked my father
fifty years after Hitler came to power, "What did you do
in the war?" for the first time and with genuine interest and
a stomach in knots. What would I hear?

By all accounts, there was no need for him to feel guilty
for having done anything dishonorable in the war, and there
weren't many things he felt sensitive about. The subject of
the Nazis was never avoided, and what he told me about
them was unambiguous: that they were the biggest criminals ever to set a jackboot on this earth. I did know that
my father was never a soldier, although he had worked as
an actor entertaining troops. I also knew vaguely that he
had been connected in some way with the plot to assassinate
Hitler in 1944, but that, too, didn't overly impress me. At
fourteen I was at an age when all older people bored me
with their constant and tedious recollections of the war. In
my world the question whether one's father was a Nazi or
not had no effect on how we viewed each other. I was
probably proud that my father had been against the Nazis,
but I know I was much prouder that he was charming to
my girlfriends and that they had a crush on him as if he
were a movie star.

Still, I had learned to stifle my curiosity. The Nazi past

remains an unresolved conflict for my parents' generation. Despite the ostensible absence of any particular taboo at home, and the fact that my parents didn't react too defensively, whenever the subject occasionally came up they still gave us to understand that there was a dangerous and troubling undercurrent in this line of inquiry, that some things were better left untouched. I often felt that the confident way my father talked about the past was too devoid of doubt, as if it was absolutely natural that he had been against the Nazis. There was no room for detailed questions, and no encouragement to probe any further. I sensed the pain and suffering behind everything he told me and his chatty openness concealed a subtle inner resistance. For him, his wartime conduct was a dead subject, it had been resolved in his mind a long time ago. He did tell me fascinating facts, Hitler jokes and anecdotes—but the largely incomprehensible "Why?" my unpsychological father couldn't tell me.

There were, of course, questions I would have liked to ask—about the Jews, for example. But I couldn't find words casual enough so that such a calamitous subject might somehow fit into a cozy dinner-table chat. Blurting, "Is it true that their gold teeth were ripped out after they were gassed? And that their hair was used for mattresses?" seemed incompatible with asking for a second helping of chocolate pudding with vanilla sauce. I think my unflappable, voluble father would have answered such questions; it was I who was afraid of the answers.

Asking one's father about such confusing and impossible matters was risky, and silence was the best protection against the fears and conflicts that might erupt into the open if the wounds of war were recklessly rubbed raw. Two major forces were at work: the fear of discovery and the desire to obey. Most Germans of my age suffered—and many still do—from the fear that they might discover something in their daddy's past that would make them despise and doubt him. There was also that continuing sense of shame, which often resulted in an attempt to separate oneself from the hated legacy by simply not wanting to know too much. This dissociation was crucial for me for a long time. Was I convincingly innocent enough? I didn't exactly believe that my genes somehow made me predisposed to mindlessly carry out despicable orders, but the German connection was disturbing enough to make me want to forget about it—despite the reassuring fact of my Lithuanian mother.

Worse still was the trait of obedience, that ubiquitous German trademark which made suppressing questions so normal that it wasn't even noticed. Where conformity is a virtue inquisition becomes a vice. The rules in most German homes were established early on, and the message was unmistakable: "Thou shalt not ask." Who would dare to bring down the wrath of a father by questioning his authority when all we do is hunger for his love and approval?

I have never met Germans of my generation who didn't have a conflict with their fathers about the past at some time in their lives. The risk of discovering a *Heil*-screamer behind a father figure who was supposed to be flawless was high, considering the overwhelming Nazi majority in Germany. None of the families I knew were in possession of that spectacular species we saw on syndicated American TV shows, the Wonder Dad who was delightfully warm and attentive, fair and patient, who played not just with sons but with daughters too, and even helped Mom in the kitchen. In our homes the father was the undisputed patriarch, unassailable and beyond any doubt. But the older we got, and the more facts we learned, the more contradictions appeared. The past crawled out sporadically, creeping into living rooms, and catching families like a spider weaving an invisible web. Not even the most virtuous human being, if he had lived through the Third Reich, could project to his children enough moral rectitude to be completely above suspicion. Did we really know who was sitting with us at the dinner table every evening, being served by our moms in aprons, and automatically getting the biggest piece of meat?

Such unvoiced conflict at home had no chance ever to be resolved completely. It didn't matter that it seemed apparent that my father genuinely wasn't a Nazi. The relative guilt or innocence of any father made little difference to me. There was still no proof, no irrefutable piece of evidence that could identify, beyond the shadow of a doubt, our fathers as either guilty or innocent. I had heard too many times that nobody knew or did anything, and I had always wondered where the real perpetrators were hiding.

Few parents attempted, let alone succeeded, in bringing the Third Reich emotionally alive for their children. And because of their failure to share with their children feelings of recognition, sorrow, regret, and even guilt, our suspicions were permitted to deepen. Few German sons and daughters have a mass murderer or a heroic anti-Nazi for a father. We live with them in a mental twilight zone. How substantial were our fathers' sins or their good deeds? We don't know. One rarely had the chance to come face to face with credible people who could testify that Dad untiringly helped Jewish neighbors or that he personally never committed any indecent acts. There are no reliable witnesses. All we children have is hope against hope. We are forced to take our parents at their word.

In families where it was obvious that the father was a

full-fledged Nazi the subject was entirely avoided. (It helps that there is no such thing as a reformed or repentant Nazi.) Usually, the children of such a man reject their father and sever almost all ties, feeling only contempt and anger—which is a form of avoidance—and thereby institutionalize their crippling relationship. Or they may defend him, spinning rationalizations and minimizing his guilt, thus reproducing their father's own repression. (There is no such thing as a Nazi who openly and freely confesses, "I am guilty.")

Can one be a good father and a horrible human being? Apparently so. But it must be difficult for a man who participated in mass killings without remorse also to be seen as a caring, devoted father in the eyes of his children. The term "good father" is frequently mentioned when Nazi criminals recollect their childhood, even when severe corporal punishment was part of it, and they are often labeled the same by their own children. On the other hand, there exist as many accounts of benevolent and beloved men who gained respect and admiration for their contributions to art and science who are seen by their children as cruel and unfit fathers.

A father's worth isn't judged by his ideology or his achievements in the outside world. My mistrust of my father was visceral and began before I could even think of him as a former *Reichsbürger*. I had to learn that I couldn't be the child I was without eliciting disappointment, ironic putdowns, and half-serious threats to be banished to a notorious detention home for "difficult" children. When I developed into the kind of daughter he didn't want, he became the father I didn't want to obey anymore and my will to criticize and find flaw with him increased. Because of my father's weakened position finding flaws wasn't difficult. My hero had become chipped around the edges and was about to topple from his pedestal. German fathers are fallen idols, which is a particularly high price for them to pay because of their need to turn their homes into private dictatorships and become mini-Führers in their own right.

Our parents were as deprived of personal power under Hitler as they were as children under their parents. In Hitler they had the continuation of a father figure, and were again reduced to children who had to obey big Papa Adolf. Both of my parents' lives fit into this pattern. My mother lacked self-esteem because she didn't play any important role at home, other than as Daddy's oldest and favorite daughter; she had no voice in her marriage either. Thus, she grabbed at her first opportunity to become a powerful and meaningful figure—motherhood. My father fared a bit better, being his mother's oldest and favorite son, and once he reached adulthood he automatically became the head of his family, and could therefore feel free to manipulate and control not only his children but his wife as well.

My father was born in Hamburg in 1912, which wasn't a good time to be a child in Germany. The Prussian principles of child rearing were crippling and cruel, full of discipline and order, corporal punishment and psychological abuse. A German boy of that time wore an emotional straitjacket. He was drilled to be tough and fearless, like a soldier, and to love his fatherland. A German boy didn't cry.

My father's parents were the quintessential "educated" middle-class Germans, the kind whose undaunted love for the Kaiser sent young men to World War I with flowers in their gun barrels, and whose support later helped the Third Reich to rise. They were pious Protestants, active in church and modest at home. My grandmother came from a puritan and distinctively North Frisian Islands family. She was clean in spirit and had a strict moral code that banned liquor and lipstick, loose talk and reckless conduct. She was trim and brisk like a terrier, wore no-nonsense clothes, smelled of lavender, and always had a handkerchief tucked into her sleeve. Her even-tempered disposition was as soothing as her piano playing, but her house, which I loved, was the only place where I felt profligate for reading comics instead of the Bible, or listening to the hit parade instead of Handel and Bach.

My grandfather was a merchant with a Polish, Jewish, and East Prussian background (he was an illegitimate child) shrouded in mystery. Less Victorian and ethereal than his wife, he was a stocky man, with a shock of white hair that stood up in all directions. He smoked big cigars, wore plaid plush slippers and suspenders, and disappeared daily to the farthest corner of their big garden to make little fires, putter around, and escape from my grandmother's constant bickering. He seemed jovial and good-natured (I was twelve when he died), and I never saw the irascible and brutal side of him that my father suffered until he was eighteen, and which accounted for their lifelong contempt for each other.

In many ways my father was an ordinary bourgeois father, typical of his generation, although he would deny it. He saw himself as one of the world's most original gifts to mankind and as an atypical German. He was embarrassed to be German and wanted to be thought of as "international." (Yet in Majorca he would shamelessly complain in broken Spanish about some "typical Spanish" inefficiency in an innately German way.) He considered himself the epitome of a modern, tolerant father who didn't beat his children the way he had been by his father (my mother did that instead, sometimes with considerable gusto) and allowed them to express themselves. On the surface he was a perfect father with a courteous and suave presence that impressed even my teachers, but I always wished that he would have looked inside my heart and helped me growing up.

He sensed that I was part of a new, threatening, colorful world to which he had only limited access and over which he had little control. Still, it was important for him not to appear old-fashioned in any way, and he wanted a full report from me about new trends in fashion, music, and lifestyles. He brought pop records home from his office and we listened to them together, and I filled him in on the latest teenage vernacular, which was a delightful new language after decades of harsh, humorless, militaristic forms of expression, and it amused him greatly. Compared with his father, who was a hard and moody man whose approval he could never win, he had come a long way, but I still wasn't allowed to do anything that cost money or that forced him to alter his plans to accommodate something as minor as a child's desire. He always came first. Nevertheless, there were fissures in his ideas about child rearing which allowed me occasionally to take advantage of his fluctuating methods. On the one hand, he said things like "As long as you put your feet under my table you do what I say"; on the other hand, he was a liberal and a pacifist who was against rearmament and for conscientious objection; he was also the one I went to when I needed justice and objectivity, things my mother had never heard of. An enthusiastic troublemaker outside (and a despot at home), he made a point of encouraging my sister and me to speak up fearlessly against injustice—as long as it was not aimed at him—and maybe that was his greatest contribution to my own character. He hated authority, having suffered under it greatly, and ignited a taste for rebellion in me, but his unfocused rage, often directed at minor, bureaucratic forms of rigidity, never transcended his need to behave like an authoritarian himself.

He always wanted to be somebody special, and thought that limelight is the only light that warms the soul and makes people love you. He had to be the center of attention and anybody he suspected of scene stealing was banned from our home, so in the end he had no real friends left. He was never an overly affectionate man, and he had trouble showing his emotions; when he tried to show love and tenderness, it came out as awkward, shy gestures as he struggled to overcome his isolation. A pinch on the cheek and a pat on the head had to do. Yet while he never ever admitted to his own fears, confusion, and vulnerability, he didn't hesitate to criticize his wife, his children, or anybody else. Most people feared his acid tongue, but nevertheless succumbed to his charm and impeccable manners. An audience always brought out his best talents. He was incredibly funny, and could entertain large groups of people with his sharp-witted repartee and priceless imitations of other people. At times arrogant and debonair, he was occasionally quite goofy, which was refreshing and endearing. We laughed a lot together. Without an audience, he was just my father, a man dressed in striped flannel pajama pants, a shaving brush in his hand, making grimaces with his foam-covered face. A man I never saw naked.

I was his favorite daughter—when I was a little girl and literally sang his tune. He hoped that I would be the one to fill his shoes and dance away to a bigger and better fate than his. But I wanted my own shoes, in my size. A woman's shoes. That's when our relationship deteriorated. I didn't choose in life what my father thought was best for him.

We had terrible shouting matches when I was between

sixteen and twenty-five years old, howling our pain into the sky like lonely wolves. I was the target for all his frustrations in his life, and only as I grew older did I understand that this destructive battle was a distorted form of love.

He never rewarded my older sister with his rage, only with condescension. She was dull and unchallenging in his eyes, afraid of him, standing in the background, silenced by his remarks about her lack of originality. I was a more formidable opponent, however, having had a savage teacher. In our fights he said ugly things a father should never say to a daughter, words that were doubtless similar in spirit to those his father had said to him when he wanted to follow his own dream and not orders.

Of all the images I have of my father, one stands out in my memory because it's so simple and peaceful. He was a passionate angler. We had a tiny cabin by a big, beautiful lake which he liked to fish in. He would sit for endless hours on the little dock he had built for himself, gazing into the soft ripples of the lake, waiting for the fish, his old-fashioned bamboo rods lined up next to him.

This normally impatient and pushy man would actually wait motionlessly for these scaly creatures to swallow his bait. He had also built a small shack at the other end of the property, hidden by old trees, and the minute we arrived he would disappear into his fortress looking the well-dressed executive and emerge minutes later wearing baggy old flannel pants smeared with dried fish slime and a few shimmering scales, crepe-soled shoes that hadn't been shined since 1947, and a broad grin. My mother was banned from the shack for good reason, and would sneak in only twice a year to snoop around and leave her mark by trying to snatch away his old clothes, hanging on rusty nails, which dated back to the forties.

It was always dim in that shack—there was only a tiny window and no electricity—and it was filled with rods, lures, eel traps, zinc buckets, tools, old gloves, knives, petroleum lamps, moldy sweaters, and one American plaid lumber jacket. I would go back there to break the boredom I felt occasionally with my sister and mother, who would lie languorously in the grass getting suntans and reading magazines.

I would quietly slip into the cool darkness and just stand around, barefoot, looking intently at all the stray objects, getting ice-cold feet from the damp cement floor, until I heard my mother or father shout, "Where's Bini?" At that point I would dart out of the shack, as if I had been caught entering a forbidden zone, and run back into the sunlight and yell, "Here!"

Life at home had an edge to it by the time I was fourteen. I was the ultimate teenager, and thought I belonged to some new human species that was rightfully destined to replace all older people on the planet. Having been born after the war, I had a strong sense of being part of a modern generation and was certain that we would soon create and define a new world where only our values, our looks, and our idols would have a place and everything else would be banned. My craving for newness was almost an obsession, and there was absolutely nothing German I wanted to copy. After all, everything German had only resulted in wars.

To my surprise and dismay, this healthy struggle for identity and separation was met with annoyance and hostility by my father and, to a lesser degree, by my mother. Early on, I developed the incurable social disease of always talking back and having to have the last word. My father shared the same affliction and our arguments were heated and endless. My parents were perplexed by my principled refusal to be obedient, and I was soon regarded as oversensitive, uncharming, and, above all, disrespectful, lost to the world of pearl necklaces, ladylike etiquette, and rich husbands.

What did they want from me? That I write a thank-you note every day for being able to live without having bombs falling on my head? Why should I be punished for having the luck of knowing that my friends and I were unlikely ever to become soldiers and widows? How did they dare to compare our lives with theirs? When they were younger they got themselves into a mess, and now they were jealous of our unconstrained life and begrudged us the opportunity to be individuals instead of cannon fodder.

I withdrew emotionally from my parents, especially my father, and relegated them to a group that included every German over fifty. I would respond to my father's hurtful sarcasm by being accusatory and insolent, which helped me to compensate for feeling misunderstood, mistreated, and unloved.

"We are not in the Hitler Youth here," I snapped at my father one day when he was canceling my allowance in order to exercise his authority "for my own good." He immediately became quiet. I had found the miracle weapon. The most perfect, custom-made, effective instrument for hardhitting insults that was guaranteed never to fail. I doubt I was alone in this: there must have been many families in which a rebellious daughter or son called their father "old Nazi" in moments of rage.

When I was twenty, my father made a crucial mistake. My parents had just moved to Majorca, and I visited them there for the first time, with my friend Tom, a rather handsome artist whose curls crept down his neck (it was 1966) and who sported a pinkish corduroy jacket with matching jeans, his idea of a formal suit. At the sight of him, something got into my father. Although he himself was dressed in an unspeakable "leisure" suit and wore white plastic shoes and an indescribable hat, he stubbornly objected to Tom's accompanying us to a nearby restaurant. "I won't come along with him looking like that," he hissed at my mother, hoping for support. For me, this was the last straw, and my anger at a father who didn't support my choices and made no real attempt to understand me exploded. "Yes, I know," I said. "Under Adolf you all had short hair and worked harder, and in the concentration camps they didn't even have hair at all. Nazi!"

His face quivered slightly and he turned pale. "That is outrageous," he said. "To call me a Nazi. Everybody knows that I was against it!" (My mother fluttered in the background, whispering, "You can't say that, Bini, that's not true," always defending him, when it didn't concern her own conflicts with him.)

"Yeah? That's what they all say. I suppose you think the whole thing is an invention anyway," I replied. I decided then that I didn't have a father anymore. We talked very little for the rest of that visit, and even less for the next fifteen years. Today, I understand my anger and disappointment much better. I was forced to give up my last idealistic notions about my daddy and it came as a shock to me. He had crossed the line I had drawn for him that separated him from his peers, and had joined the ranks of ordinary, conservative pensioners. I had never trusted his generation and now I couldn't even trust him anymore, now that he had shown himself to be irretrievably German after all.

It was, of course, unfair of me to call him a Nazi and to

mercilessly criticize his every gesture or opinion that without the burden of an ignominious past would have been
forgiven with less emotional drama. I couldn't be the judge
of his political past, or his life; I could only judge him the
way a daughter can, with blinkered eyes. For self-righteous
moralizers, entertaining troops could be seen as a form of
complicity because it gave moral support to Hitler's soldiers. He never took strong measures to oppose the regime,
such as leaving the country, going underground, or joining
a resistance group. For him, working as an entertainer was
the least compromising activity he could find. Yet he was
willing to risk his life. He didn't have a leader's mentality,
but he offered his assistance whenever he saw a chance to
act on his conscience. When I asked him why he had become
involved in the Hitler assassination plot, he said simply, "I
once did something for the Nazis [he voted for them in
1933], now I wanted to do something against them."

More than anything else, he acted according to his character, before, during, and after the Nazis. That he was born
into that time was his fate, and that alone can't be construed
as a crime. Since I'll never know for sure what he did or
didn't do in the war, there is only one area in which I can
judge whether or not he acted responsibly. Was he able to
transform his invaluable experience into an emotionally and
politically relevant lesson for his children? Could he com-
municate the message that something like the Holocaust
must never happen again, and that we would bear the burden of the sins of his generation as well as the responsibility
of avoiding their recurrence? Unfortunately, he was never
interested in politics, and the same impulse and talent to
shirk loathsome duties that kept him from cooperating with
Hitler later made him reluctant to participate actively with

passion and conviction in any cause. He was afraid of depth and dedication, and was never willing to go to the bottom of things; he lacked the psychological insight for that.

As I learned more about my father, I had difficulty separating my father the person from my father the citizen of the Third Reich. Where did the Nazi legacy end? This problem lay at the root of my troubling and ambivalent relationship with him. Were his answers to my questions satisfactory? Yes and no. I had the impossible dream every child probably has once in a lifetime that can never be realized. I was searching for the man he once was. I wanted to be a time-traveler and meet him as a young man without a past, as a person, not a father, released from the burden of having to live like a saint in the shadow of guilt. For myself, I wanted to be released from the burden of being a daughter.

He wasn't getting any younger, and this would be my chance to confront him—real *gemütlich*, over a couple of drinks, on a sunny Mediterranean island, surrounded by olive and almond trees. I went to see him to find out, at last, how he is able to live with his history, how it was that he came to serve Führer and fatherland as a singing actor and troop entertainer for German soldiers in Poland, Belgium, Holland, France, and Denmark. I wanted his story—from the beginning.

"I had the impression that you wanted to avoid the subject," says my father, without blinking an eye. "Since I had daughters I guess I didn't make a big deal out of it. I thought it's not interesting for girls." He leans back in his rattan chair, crosses his tanned legs, and sips his Campari. We are in Ibiza, the beautiful Spanish hot spot for the incurably chic, adorably young, and incorrigibly rich—and also the temporary home of Karl-Heinz Reichel. We are sitting on a spacious terrace. A father, a daughter, and the German past. A sunlit drama with two people in bathing suits.

My father, now in his late seventies, is still a good-looking man, tall and rather slim. He always wears a hat because of his thinning hair, and his beard is neatly clipped and slightly dyed. He has prepared for our confrontation, our first talk in over ten years—he's brought a big photo album and several pieces of paper—"evidence" of the part he played in the Hitler assassination plot.

At first I'm shocked when my father tells me he voted for the Nazis with great enthusiasm in 1933. He had never mentioned it before. To me, every person who didn't hate Hitler in 1933 was categorically a flaming Nazi. An unrealistic assumption I would have to revise.

He remembers the chaos: "My father was a merchant and had just formed a company when Black Friday occurred. He had to fight to survive. Around this time the words 'National Socialists' came up more often. My parents were very Christian people and I was sent to the Bible club. More and more people left the club and it was said that they joined the storm troopers. These people were mostly poor and they did it for the pay and the food they received.

"There was a lot of violence in the streets—people in cars and on motorbikes were robbed at night—and I had a bike. Hitler made a lot of promises that made sense to us. We all thought that the death penalty would stop all that and that Hitler was quite a guy.

"Also, my political background was strictly German National Party, like the majority. For generations my family was faithful to the Kaiser and they believed in regaining order and godliness. The most threatening group was the

Social Democrats. I couldn't even whisper that name at home. They stood for everything decadent and subversive.

"I was a young man and much more interested in girls and playing tennis and hockey than in politics. Not once at that time did I hear anything critical about the regime from anybody. I had no 'warners.' The concentration camps of those years were labor camps, with few Jews among them, and acceptable to most people."

Karl-Heinz Reichel wanted to become an actor, and why not? He was a dark, handsome man, with melancholic brown eyes—a real heartthrob with slick manners. Acting was looked upon as a seedy profession by religious people like his parents, however, so he moved out. He went to Berlin to take acting lessons from a half-Czech, half-Yugoslav teacher, who also introduced him to artists who were different from most of the people he knew in Hamburg.

He must have had talent and I know he was very musical, which landed him good but light parts in provincial theaters between Hamburg and Berlin before the war, mostly those of the bon vivant who gets the girl. His sense of self-parody prevented him from taking himself too seriously as an actor (he wanted to direct anyway), but he showed me excellent reviews which were neatly clipped and pasted into a big book together with old photographs, original theater programs, lyrics for early postwar pop songs, and other memorabilia.

Karl-Heinz Reichel began to see things differently in the years 1935–37. "I heard that the Jews who were members of the posh tennis club I belonged to were asked to resign. And slowly stories from the concentration camps began to leak out. Torture was mentioned, and I was particularly suspicious that there were so many prisoners 'shot while escaping.' Nobody would try to escape from the notoriously guarded camps. I didn't believe it. Then they started to take away the companies of Jewish businessmen. My father told me that. I must say, I wasn't for the Nazis anymore. In the last election in 1937–38—there was only the NSDAP—I didn't vote for the Nazis but didn't have the guts to tell my parents."

My father brushes away a few imaginary crumbs from the table and goes on. "There were two occasions when the Nazis didn't seem so bad to me. One was the Olympic Games in Berlin in 1936, a masterfully organized spectacle everybody loved—the French marched in with raised arms—and the other one the visit of Chamberlain to Munich. In my eyes the British were traditionally the greatest politicians. If they came to Hitler, then there must be something good about the National Socialist movement.

"But then came the annexation of Austria and the attack on Czechoslovakia in 1938, and I thought, 'That man won't stop, he wants the whole world.' I mean, I read in the papers that we were declared a *Volk ohne Raum* [people without a space], but this . . ." He gives a brief Hitler imitation, barking out slogans in the Führer's imitable guttural voice, a favorite with elderly Germans.

"I began to listen to Hitler's speeches with great interest. I didn't always comprehend them. He was very cunning and never mentioned war. He said exactly what politicians say nowadays: that we don't want a war. We also don't have "war" ministers anymore, as we did under the Kaiser; today they are called "defense" ministers. Hitler said, 'Because we want to prevent a war, we have to rearm'—just as they say today. Therefore, I didn't find his speeches necessarily alarming in terms of moving toward a war."

Now my father is talking about 1938. He was living in

Berlin, the *Reichshauptstadt* [capital]. He had just finished an engagement at a theater on the Kurfürstendamm, and was rather content with his life, when something unforgettable happened—the *Kristallnacht*, a night of shattering glass, burning synagogues, and plundering hordes of SA men, an organized and open pogrom that left no doubt about Hitler's plans. The SA and their civilian helpers smashed the windows of Jewish stores all over Germany, placing viciously grinning Brownshirts in front of the wreckage holding signs that read "*Kauft nicht bei Juden.*"

"I walked through the city the next morning," my father says, "and was very shocked and very angry. What I saw, besides the smashed windows, straightened me out forever. I witnessed Gestapo men taking Jews away from their houses, among them a very old man wearing an Iron Cross from World War I. They beat him up brutally and ripped off the Cross. After the *Kristallnacht*, I was sure that the rest of the world, especially America, would get involved. I thought, 'This is it. The Nazis are not getting away with this one.' But nothing happened."

My father stops and leans back. It is late afternoon but still hot. He is tired, and also a little nervous. His right hand sweeps over the table, but there are no crumbs. He looks thoughtful. Yet, while telling me tales of terror and assaults on humanity, his voice stays flat and reportorial, while his face remains expressionless. Like so many of his peers, he expresses only a contorted form of pity and sadness about the senseless slaughter of millions, and his account sometimes sounds callous and is spiked with irony and cynicism. His moment of outcry had long since passed, and his feelings of pain and outrage were smothered and couldn't be reactivated anymore. Whatever tears he might have shed, he must have shed them in private.

The lines were sharply drawn for Karl-Heinz Reichel in 1938. This was a regime he didn't want to support anymore, but a regime he couldn't escape. Open resistance was impossible. One wrong word and the Gestapo was knocking at the door. The only way to survive without active participation was to withdraw from the system, which was as impossible as separating Adolf Hitler from his mustache. Citizens of the Reich were under permanent surveillance. There was always an eager Brownshirt around, reminding people to join the Party or the Hitler Youth, to donate money or clothes to the cause.

"I wasn't a political person," my father says after a long silence, "and I wasn't even interested in the system, because I wasn't a super-patriot or a war nut. Heroic stories from World War I and all this glorification of fighting and shooting wasn't for me. My father served in World War I in Russia, but he hated the military and wasn't crazy about fighting either. I can't say I'm a courageous person. One thing was for sure, there was no way I would ever be a soldier fighting at the front. I would have avoided it at any cost. Oh God, no!" He looks up and clasps his hands together.

"Not wanting to be a soldier was probably looked upon as dishonorable, but I didn't care. In my circles not wearing a uniform was an honor. Besides, not wanting to be a soldier wasn't exactly an ideological decision. I saw the soldiers who came back severely wounded, blind, shot to pieces. No, it was nothing but naked fear. Every man for himself. I didn't feel guilty that other men fought at the front. Everyone wearing a uniform was a stranger to me, spiritually."

War broke out in September 1939. Karl-Heinz Reichel was called up for the draft in 1940, but was deferred when he invented a bone-marrow disease backed up by an old hockey injury. He was called up again at the end of 1940, and couldn't escape this time. The Wehrmacht wanted him on the home front and in uniform. But he arranged, through an old colleague, to be sent with a theater ensemble to tour the front as a troop entertainer for the Wehrmacht in the occupied countries.

The tour started in Warsaw in October 1940. "I was in absolute opposition to the regime," he says, "and so was the rest of our group." How, then, could he justify entertaining a group of predatory German soldiers in an occupied country? How does it feel to be on the side of the occupiers just by nationality?

My father doesn't blame the Wehrmacht. "The soldiers were poor devils who were happy to have some hours of entertainment. I didn't hate them. We were only actors and somehow in the same boat with them. I was glad to be an actor and not a soldier. There was no choice in the Third Reich anyway. The most important thing to me was to make clear that I wasn't a Nazi in the occupied countries, to get across that we were just doing our job as actors. Wherever we went we had contact with active anti-Nazis.

"On the surface I had quite a good life. I stayed in the best hotels and had the best food. But most of the time I was afraid. We had to be careful.

"I didn't give one pfennig for my life. Anything could happen, because I knew there was no justice in the Third Reich. The worst thing about it was that innocent people were constantly killed—apart from the Jews—because of stupid mistakes, mix-ups, and denunciations. I was terrified, but my attitude was that I wanted to do something, but please, can't someone tell me where and how?"

In Poland in 1941, German soldiers showed him photos of trenches filled with corpses and told him gruesome stories of concentration camps. He and a friend managed to get permission to visit a concentration camp near Lublin. They wanted to see whether the Germans would let them in and what they would find. It was a small labor camp with old people and children. They didn't see any shower rooms or crematories.

Not even the fluffy Italian and Japanese comedies—the *Kultur* was purged of anything that contained the spirit of freedom or came from an enemy country—could cover up the deteriorating morale of the troupe—and their audience. The invasion of Russia was slowly turning into a catastrophe, and between their lifeless, leaden performances, the actors and soldiers listened to the news from the front on the radio.

"I'm telling you, we weren't in it for an Academy Award. It was a question of survival. The crimes of the Nazis were known to us by now. There was no turning back anymore. It had to end disastrously. I knew that nothing would turn out good in this nightmare."

The sun is slowly setting, turning the Ibizian sky into all shades of purple-pink. The crickets start chirping. We are both hungry. My father is fidgeting in his chair. He wants to take a break. He ends the conversation with an abrupt "I'll tell you the rest tomorrow."

The next afternoon, we sit together in the same arrangement—same time, same chairs, same drinks, and same wild swimming trunks on his tanned body. I can keep in good humor about this exasperating mixture of habit and compulsion because I escaped it.

But something is new today—his tranquillity, his modesty. Known as a hyperactive, ranting, smug charmer, he is suddenly simple and sober. Perhaps it was the tape recorder that made him feel important, and helped him, for a fleeting moment, to be in touch with himself. Certainly he took me more seriously than ever before, for he let me be his chronicler.

I still hadn't heard the story of the nerve-wracking day of July 20, 1944, the glorious and only day of massive, organized German resistance—a failure, but at least a try. Instead of Hitler, hundreds of innocent men were shot and their families persecuted in an incredibly brutal reaction that lasted into the final days of the war.

"You know what?" he begins. "I find it embarrassing to talk about it. Since five out of ten people say they were in the resistance and fought the Nazis, one is surprised that the Third Reich could happen in the first place. It's just too embarrassing."

After finishing a tour in 1943 in Denmark, he received another draft order, but thanks to connections with people who happened to be anti-Nazi he managed to get a job as an announcer and entertainment producer at the Reichs Rundfunk in Berlin.

"In July '44," my father continues, "a certain Herr von Rieck, whom I had met at a party where people had talked very openly about resistance against Hitler, informed me of Operation Valkyrie, the Hitler assassination plot. [He shows me a crumpled paper with his handwritten name.] By the way, I never heard from Herr von Rieck again. I'm sure it wasn't his real name. Anyway, he knew that I was in opposition and so approached me with their plans. After the success of the assassination, the Rundfunk was to be immediately occupied and two announcers were to read a text prepared by the new government. I was to be one of those announcers.

"Now, for the person who would be contacting me after the assassination, I had to have a special identification, one that would be inconspicuous for the Nazis and SS officers who had tight control over the Rundfunk. The item that would show that I was the right man was my fake identity card in Wehrmacht uniform as an officer. The point was that I was a civilian and had never worn a uniform—that fake identity card would be the clue. On my Wehrmacht papers, which every German man possessed, it was noted that I was a civilian, which could be checked by my contact. I hadn't started working yet, and it was arranged for me to borrow a uniform and for the picture to be taken. So I had my identity card and could enter the Rundfunk. In my position it was normal to wear civilian clothes, so nobody was suspicious of the photo."

He shows me a picture labeled "Ausweis Nr. 871, Gruppe Z," dated July 13, 1944–January 31, 1945. The photo is silly and I burst into laughter. There is something about those imposing hats with their high brims that makes even a handsome, naïve-looking man like my father resemble Adolf Eichmann. He's mildly amused too, but he doesn't share the strange mixture of hilarity and terror I feel whenever I come across pictures of those pompous, conceited-looking creatures in their ridiculous riding pants, or when I see film footage of the marching, swastika-swinging, square-jawed, thin-lipped SA men and their stupefied expressions. It's vanity that keeps him from laughing—and after all he was a contemporary, personally linked to the aesthetic look of the Third Reich.

Of course, the assassination failed, and when the word was out that Adolf Hitler was still alive, Karl-Heinz Reichel was terrified. He looked feverishly for a plausible explanation in case they investigated the broadcasting station. He hadn't done anything, but complicity was enough.

"I started to think about it day and night and grew numb

with fear. I wished that I had never even known about the whole assassination business. They arrested about ten Nazis from the Rundfunk right away, but they weren't satisfied. Suddenly, in November '44, the Gestapo came and accused me of having known something. They said they positively knew that someone from the station was informed and that it all boiled down to me, so why not confess right away?

"At that time I was a nervous wreck and taking a lot of uppers, so I could give one of my better performances ever. I played the outraged upright Nazi and snapped at them, 'How dare you insult me like that? To do something against my Führer . . . Excuse me, I'm busy.'

"I stomped out of the office right into the bathroom, where I threw up. Without all the pills, I would have cracked up right in front of them."

Life in the bunker of the Reichs Rundfunk was tough enough as it was. The daily news program *Der Zeitspiegel* was usually preproduced, but beginning in 1943 "live" commentaries were occasionally added as updates.

"When it was our turn to read 'live,' " my father says, "two SS men came in—very friendly and casual—shook hands and all that. Then they took out their revolvers and put them on the table with understated significance." He laughs and adds, "And I mean not to let me try out the revolver or to show me the brand name. Needless to say, we read the news just as it came in, lies or not. When we were finished, they picked up their revolvers, said 'Heil Hitler' politely, and walked out."

It sounds almost funny now, and he has a little smirk while telling me the story, but of course it was really hell. By 1944, it had begun to dawn on many Germans that the war was lost. The bombing of German cities started in 1943 and inflicted the bitter reality of war on the German people.

The newscasters had to be available around the clock, and weren't allowed to go to bomb shelters. "I was afraid and the future looked black and hopeless. I knew I lived in a land among war criminals," my father says.

The search for soothing illusions during the last part of the war was desperate. There was always a party somewhere, with lots of alcohol. Someone always had enough connections to supply some schnapps. Drunk or not, what did it matter?

Even the rare moments of entertainment were affected by the war. Equipped with a good voice, my father had sometimes dubbed foreign films. Quite a crooner himself, he had even been proud to lend *Der Bingel* his speaking voice. "But after America joined the war," he goes on, "English words weren't allowed anymore, not even in lyrics, and they asked me to also sing Bing Crosby's film songs from *Double or Nothing* in German." He sings a few bars of "The Natural Thing to Do." "I could do that well, but it was so ridiculous that I refused. The movie was then withdrawn from the theaters."

This is the kind of memory my father likes to preserve. It flatters his self-image and suggests the kind of talent he could never express in either Nazi Germany or in the artless pop-artistic contortions of postwar Germany in the 1950s.

"Suddenly, in January '45, another investigation of the Rundfunk was announced. I got cold feet and wanted to leave." An actress friend's family doctor helped him out of that dilemma. After a medical examination, he was able to take a leave of absence for two months and immediately fled into the Austrian mountains.

"When the Americans came in March of '45, I rushed down to their headquarters and told them that I was an anti-Nazi. The American lieutenant, a native German who had emigrated in '33, revealed to me that he belonged to the CIC [Counter-Intelligence Corps]. After they investigated my case and I was cleared, they wanted me to screen conversations of some Germans whom they suspected of being from the SS. I was only too willing to work for them; I had feelings of revenge against the Nazis, especially the SS. So I followed them around—in civilian clothes—sat down next to them with a newspaper, and kept tabs on everything unusual.

"One thing I became aware of immediately. The Americans knew from the first day of capitulation that one day it would be them against the Russians and that the war wasn't over. They were looking for experts on Communism, and the people they picked could have been war criminals, it didn't matter. They were all released, supplied with papers and money, and sent to East Germany, Buenos Aires, and so on. I saw people who had worn SS uniforms—I could tell by the imprint that the removed oak leaves had left on their uniform jackets—suddenly prancing around, smoking American cigarettes, and chewing gum. After that assignment I was hired for the broadcasting station Rot-Weiss-Rot in Salzburg and stayed until the end of '45."

A wave of denunciation started when the Allies staged the denazification farce. My father was suddenly accused of having been an SS *Oberscharführer*. He couldn't work for two months until his case was cleared. "I still received threatening letters from National Socialists who came from my parents' neighborhood, even into the early '50s, saying 'You better watch your children . . . ,' stuff like that."

My father still sees the Third Reich as a tragic accident rather than a welcomed, celebrated regime. "A crew of people came to power at a certain time. If they had killed Hitler earlier, a war could have been prevented.

"For me, National Socialism is Hitler's invention. But nevertheless it contained about twenty percent of the elements the Germans very much wanted, such as order, discipline, compulsory labor, obedience. But speaking of the typical German national character: it has a lot of flaws but isn't too unusual either.

"I would say that the British have the same traits we are talking about, but it is also a country where National Socialism could never have happened. The two countries where it was possible are the ones where it actually happened: Germany and Italy. It happened in Italy because the Italians are cowards and too lazy to rebel against anything, and in Germany because the Germans aren't cowardly enough—they are too courageous. They knew that they didn't have the right to kill people and take everything away from them. But I think that these character traits are mostly a result of rearing; we aren't born with them."

Did the Germans know what was going on? He shrugs his shoulders and says ironically, "When people say they 'didn't know a thing,' they mean that they didn't know *how* the people were killed in the concentration camps. Everybody knew about their existence and that people were killed there. We heard about the gas much later, and still couldn't really imagine it. I can confirm that we all lived in fear. The brutality of the Nazis is responsible for people shutting their mouths. I think more people might have rebelled otherwise."

He doesn't believe in collective guilt, and he doesn't feel personally guilty either. "I voted for Hitler at a time when I didn't know him. For you younger people it's hard to understand the fascination for Hitler. You're a different generation that knows from the start who he was and how it all developed. It isn't that simple and objectivity is not possible. Yes, he was a brutal man but he didn't say total rubbish all the time and what he ultimately did he didn't dare to spell out. I must say, reading *Mein Kampf* much later, one could have known better. That book is like a script. He staged many scenes . . ."

Are the Germans now "denazified"? Did they learn? He shakes his head. "Without the *Persil-Schein* [slang for the denazification certificate given by the Allies to all Party members and people in high positions, something like "Ivory Snow ticket"], everything would be exactly the same today in Germany. On all levels. There are Nazis in high positions just the same today."

Karl-Heinz Reichel is his old clever self as he wraps it up. "Everything that was good in the Third Reich wasn't new, and everything that was new wasn't good. Actually, economically the war had advantages. It wasn't bad that we had to start anew. Germany looks much nicer now— except for Dresden maybe."

Toward the end of our conversation, leafing through his photo album, I see a picture of my father as a little boy, around 1916, during a summer vacation with a group of other boys. A picture of sweet, mischievous, grinning faces, with curious eyes. Regular kids in sailor suits. They might have heard the word "war" at home—some might even have lost their fathers—but "war" was a word without horror, signifying a glorious event full of victorious stories which wouldn't stop even after Germany was defeated. There were no ruins yet, no burning skies and crashing bombs, no gas chambers and organized genocide. War was part of life.

I ask my father about regrets, about bitterness for the stolen years. The answer comes a shade too hastily: "No, no. That I survived all that . . . that's the miracle."

I don't believe it. I look at the picture again. Did those innocent little boys know that their lives would be forever linked with terror and Holocaust? Did they have any idea that war would alter their country's destiny, history, and geography? That the years when they were young men would also be the years that will be remembered as history's greatest extinction of body and spirit? Their fate seems inescapable—a historically predetermined layout—condemned to be executed. Victims? Perpetrators?

No, I don't believe that there were no stolen years, no destroyed lives. But I do understand that it is unbearably sad to realize the incredible damage of heart and soul the war left behind, making them prisoners of a time, of a country.

They have to protect their youth, their proof of existence. There are far worse horrors, of course, yet it's depressing to have nothing left to show from one's youth but a scrapbook of war, memorabilia marked with bloodstains, evoking pain rather than happiness. War caught them when they were ready to explore life. Instead they were lined up in uniforms and taught to shoot at their brothers. The choice was survive or die. No matter which they chose, they were condemned to pain and loss.

When I was finally able to ask my father, "What did you do in the war?" it was a small victory over fear and obedience. By putting the ghosts of the past into perspective, I was able to keep them alive without feeling threatened by them. But asking questions was more than the triumph of curiosity over authority, and of the awakening of historical consciousness over social amnesia. It was a form of liberation, a step out of childhood and into a more equal relationship between a father and a daughter. My father handed me a second chance to confront his generation's legacy; this time it was a fair encounter. It isn't any easier to take, but now that the silence has been broken it's no longer a threatening shadow either. There is no solution to the conflicts between my father and me. I have admiration and respect for the way he tried to live his life during a time I am forever grateful for having escaped. It doesn't matter that even with my new willingness to understand, some questions will remain unanswered. We both have to live with it.

# 4

# *And How About You, Mom?*

When I think about my mother I think about beauty and pain. She looked perfect, the incarnation of femininity—soft, voluptuous curves; elegance, grace, and glamour—and fit into her era, the fifties, as naturally as the gloves, perky hats, and boxy little handbags that were the hallmark of a real lady. Her pain wasn't so visible, however. It was locked away, hidden from her husband and her children and often from herself; only her accent betrayed the source of a flaw she felt deeply. She was a Lithuanian refugee, cut off from her homeland, her family, and her language. This sense of displacement had become her psychological prison, and she transformed it over the years into such a comfortable residence that she had trouble escaping it because she forgot to install a keyhole.

How my mother ended up in Germany is a story of fate, love, and, most of all, war. She had never intended to stay in Germany; in fact, she hadn't chosen to leave her homeland in the first place. But the very definition of "homeland" had always been ambiguous for my mother. Born and raised in Latvia (in Liepāja, a port on the Baltic Sea), she nonetheless considered herself purely Lithuanian since her parents had been born there and had come from established Lithuanian families. She had a Lithuanian passport, went to a Lithuanian school, and had the status of a permanent resident in Latvia. Already she was a visitor in a strange land.

In 1939, under a secret protocol to the Hitler-Stalin pact, the Red Army began occupying strategic towns in the three independent Baltic states (Estonia, Latvia, and Lithuania) and rounding up people for deportation to labor camps in Russia. My mother's worried and protective father wanted to get his two oldest daughters, eighteen-year-old Luzie and my nineteen-year-old mother, out of Latvia and sent them over the border to live with Lithuanian relatives in Kaunas. After the Russians annexed Lithuania in 1940, they still felt safe enough to remain, but in early 1941 the girls were urged by their relatives to flee to the West. Luzie had fallen in love with a Lithuanian Communist and wanted to stay, but on February 7—three days after the Russians had confiscated her passport—my mother decided to risk the hazardous escape over the Polish border into East Prussia. After weeks of interrogations by the Nazis, she arrived in Berlin, branded with two capital letters that stood for a cruelly fitting name invented by bureaucracy: DP, displaced person.

My mother recalls, "This escape, organized by the Catholic Church and the Lithuanian resistance, was such a spectacular and reckless stunt, but I had no idea how dangerous it was because I was so young and so naïve," and she smiles as if she can't imagine that it was actually she who found herself within twenty-four hours in a different world. "The

Nazis I met in Königsberg were the worst pigs of all the ones I've ever seen. They greeted me at the border with a vicious 'What does this filthy riffraff want here? You are from Lithuania? That's all we need!' I'll never forget that humiliation."

But like most Eastern European refugees, my mother saw Berlin as only a temporary address. Consumed by home-sickness and feeling out of place in this nazified nation, she yearned to be the sheltered daughter again, counting the days until she could go back home. On the other hand, Berlin was a fascinating melting pot, a genuinely cosmo-politan city with an indomitable spirit that couldn't be en-tirely suppressed by the Nazis, and my mother loved the humor and tolerance of the Berliners. Life in Berlin still had some glamour in the early forties, especially in the chic, slightly bohemian scene of mostly foreigners and a few select Germans. Like all pretty girls, my mother was invited out a lot, shown around, and exposed to the intense, plea-sure-seeking life before the deluge. She began to enjoy her new independence—she started taking German lessons and signed up for drawing classes at the Academy of Art. "I had a wonderful time in Berlin; looking back, the best of my life. I was so hungry for life and grabbed everything I could get and didn't want to see the darkness of the times," she says, sighing. But deep down her only ambition was to leave this hostile country that treated foreigners like para-sites who undeservedly ate their way through the rich and glorious National Socialist pie.

We sit on the terrace of her charming little apartment, from which we can see a sliver of the Mediterranean. Look-ing at this full-figured, perky woman in her late sixties, with her fashionable bangs and still shapely legs, it's hard to imagine that she once was the skinny, homesick young

woman with a wistful smile who is depicted in the photos
she was able to save. She is excited about talking about the
past, and I can finally make up for the many times I was
impatient and didn't know where to put the recollections
of a refugee mother.

My parents met in 1941 at a party in Berlin, and it was
immediately apparent that by looks alone they were a match
made in heaven. Moreover, she was impressed with his
candor and his entertaining personality, and he was smitten
by this classy-looking creature whose helpless femininity
was so appealing to the protective knight in him. They had
no difference of opinion about the Nazis, and what was
unclear to my mother—which was a lot—he explained to
her. Both agreed that the Nazis were despicable creeps, and
they spoke longingly of the day when the war would be
over.

They moved in together in early 1943 and because she
soon became pregnant they started to think about marriage
so she could get papers and stay in Germany. Naturally,
before getting a marriage license and being considered worthy enough of a precious eligible German man, my mother
not only had to produce proof of Aryan descent for three
generations but was also subjected to a thoroughly humiliating physical and mental examination by nasty Nazi
officials. "I was ordered to appear before an all-male committee that seemed to be happy to see a young woman; from
all directions I heard heels clicking together and young men
barking, 'Heil Hitler.' I had to bend my head down and
they pulled my hair and looked at the roots and asked, 'Are
they *echt*?' To which I replied rather freshly, 'It's not a wig,
is it?' "

My mother was three months pregnant when she was
married in Hamburg in May 1943. This partially explains

why the bride in the wedding picture looks so pale in her extravagant white satin gown. Ideology explains the rest. Obeying a mother's request—his parents paid for the lavish wedding—my father talked his young wife into accommodating her new mother-in-law for one day by making this a lipstick-free and nail-polish-free German wedding (this was also in accordance with the Führer's wishes—a German woman doesn't wear makeup). Yet after the wedding it was back to red—to my grandmother's dismay. My grandfather and my father's sister and brother, however, thought that the new wife who spoke broken German and couldn't cook an egg was simply a treasure.

And my mother didn't score so badly in the eyes of her own family by falling in love with my father. A German husband was looked upon as a good catch, for Germany had always been synonymous with *Kultur* and refinement, a vision that couldn't be distorted by the Nazis. Although my father would never meet any of them in person, he was assured of his Lithuanian in-laws' approval.

In the summer of 1943, the bombing raids on German cities reached their height and my mother had to be evacuated. She decided to go back to Latvia and was overjoyed to bear her first child surrounded by family and friends. She returned to Germany that December—this time to Hamburg—after my father sent her a telegram saying that their Berlin apartment had been bombed out and that all their belongings were in ashes. "I had planned to stay but by that time the Russians had started to move in and the Germans were moving out, and since I unfortunately was German because of my marriage, my father was afraid and urged me—for the second time in my life—to leave my country."

Hamburg was worse than Berlin. Having a little daughter

didn't assuage my mother's painful feeling that she was a homeless refugee again. How did she ever wind up in that red brick house in a dull suburb of Hamburg just in time for the RAF's nerve-racking bombing raids in 1944? Why was she at the mercy of a basically good but strict mother-in-law who made her feel that her housewifely qualities were lousy and her looks too fancy while her husband who had dumped her there led a relatively amusing life, working at the Reichs Rundfunk in Berlin and going to parties with seductive actresses?

Eager to conform, to please, and to prove that she had earned that precious privilege of living in relative luxury and safety, she tried to transform herself into a demure daughter-in-law, deferential and useful. A gregarious, fun-loving woman who liked to dance and flirt, she would spend the next year and a half immersed in activities like washing diapers, scrubbing floors, and seeking shelter from Allied bombs. She would race frantically down to the basement, suitcase and baby in tow, and then sit and wait until the earth stopped trembling and the sirens signaled the departure of the bombers. Although her heart was pounding, she would still manage to sing a soothing lullaby or rock little Sylvie in her arms.

"This helplessness of being at someone's mercy was the worst," she says. "At the front you have a weapon, so at least you have the illusion that it's a fight in which you can defend yourself, but with the bombs . . . After a time this kind of life became so normal to me that I didn't realize how crazy it actually was. I couldn't even think about whether there might be a country on this planet where life was *not* the way it was in Germany. We were all sucked in by the dynamic of survival and lived one day at a time."

Apart from this hectic schedule, for my mother the war

years meant life in the slow line. Since as many as seven adults and four children lived in my grandmother's over-crowded house (including my Aunt Trude, her husband, and their three children, who were also bombed out), noth-ing was more vital—other than saving one's life—than or-ganizing the meals. My mother spent many hours every day standing patiently in line behind young and old women, clutching in her hands the precious food stamps that meant meager rations of milk, bread, egg powder, and other trea-sures, until her lower back ached. Not much disrupted the somber mood other than the occasional reports of who had been bombed out and whose husband or son had been killed or was visiting from the front. No one dared to say what they really felt about a regime that failed to protect its citizens from foreign bombing raids and from a war whose outcome was by now predictably dire. There was agony behind the weary silence as well as numbing uncertainty: How much longer will it last? Are our men still alive? The women exchanged glances, dark with fear. They were allies in their suffering, and they did what women always do in times of war. They hoped and they waited. "I was praying that the occupiers would come soon," my mother remem-bers. "I hoped for the Americans and was very disappointed when it became clear that the English were closer to Ham-burg. Maybe it was because of the stories we were hearing about the Americans, who were giving chocolate and cig-arettes to the population in the south of Germany. The English," she says, laughing, "were stingy and reserved."

Despite her unhappiness, pregnancy and motherhood provided an inestimable advantage for my mother. She wasn't recruited for dirty work. While most women her age had to help the Führer's war effort by working in the ar-maments industry, she was spared having to operate anti-aircraft guns or stand on the assembly line, wearing overalls and a knotted scarf around her head, putting finishing touches on hand grenades. She insists that she would have resisted it at any cost because she felt no desire whatsoever to lift a finger for a crazy war or for a country she didn't love (besides simply not being the type that would slave away in a dingy factory surrounded by tough-talking proletarians and forced-labor workers from the occupied countries).

For most women who did work, the end of the war also meant the end of their careers, and many regretted it, no matter how tedious and underpaid the work might have been. The battered men came home and would have none of their wives' sudden awakening of independence which posed a threat to their already damaged self-esteem, while the women often couldn't understand why working should all of a sudden be a man's prerogative again. Yet the majority of them complied and returned, half grudgingly, half relieved, to where they had come from before the war, and would remain in the kitchen all through the fifties. (It was a crucial mistake, as their daughters would point out to them later.) "I was so happy that my husband and my child were alive. We wanted to enjoy peace, and when we sat together we talked about what we could do, not what was," explains my mother.

For German women, however, this worldwide trend of retreating into the safety of one's home was, regardless of its convenience, psychologically as well as physically far more stressful than it was for women elsewhere. They were expected not only to rebuild their country but also to clean up their minds. They are legendary for having fared spectacularly with bricks and muscles, for their iron wills and unsurpassed endurance. They postponed indefinitely the questions of guilt and participation in a murderous regime.

One irritating fact has puzzled me for years. Why is it that, for the most part and for the longest time, mothers were miraculously excluded from the suspicion of complicity which few fathers seemed to escape? Mothers added the feminine touch to wars—they never made them. My anger and suspicion—and that of my friends—were always directed at the men. They made the wars while the women had to clean up the mess. Men had the guns, dropped the bombs. They invented concentration camps and they carried out the efficient mass killings. The few notorious female camp guards and the countless numbers of women in minor administrative positions couldn't change that. Yet women were citizens of the Third Reich too and were not without influence. If it's true that behind every great man is a great woman, isn't it true then that behind every Nazi was a female Nazi?

I suppose it didn't matter to me whether women were Nazis, because they were always the nurturing, protective homemakers who couldn't kill a fly. I simply trusted women more, and I gave my mother the benefit of the doubt because my relationship with her was much more affectionate and loving than the one that I had with my father. I thought war was something she suffered as an innocent, abused bystander.

"I'm not German," she always insisted, even after living twenty-five years in the country of her husband. This was a fact that not only automatically excluded her from any connection with German guilt, which is understandable, but also disqualified her as a reliable chronicler with a coherent and distinctive political view. The Nazis were ugly, she never liked them, didn't vote for them, and that was that. She had nothing to come to terms with. "I married a

German, that's all; I don't feel related or close to anything German, and that is not suppression, it's a genuine feeling," she says firmly, and I know there is no way to get her to rethink this sentiment. However, since she lived in the country at the time when the Holocaust was about to take its most heinous form, she was forced to take a moral stand. "I remember most vividly how Jews were pushed from the sidewalks of the streets in Berlin. It was painful for me to see that people can walk by the young and the old and just push them out of their way. Once I saw a young girl wrapped in an oversized coat with a yellow star on it. She was so utterly sad and looked down at her feet while she was rushing by. This sadness is impossible to describe with words, maybe you could paint these faces. All I thought was that it could have been me with another star. What if my parents had been gassed or killed by the Germans? I think I would hate them until the end of my life."

Repression and forgetting were made easier for the women because they could hide comfortably behind the "weaker sex" role. Many thought of themselves as exploited, manipulated, and credulous victims of National Socialist indoctrination, citing how the misogynist regime reduced them to breeders, homemakers, and churchgoers. (The Nazis fired all married women from their jobs and made birth control illegal.) To accept this innocence by gender, however, is a disservice to women's rights. Claudia Koonz, author of the brilliant and provocative book *Mothers in the Fatherland*, concludes that "far from being helpless, or even innocent, women made possible a murderous state" because "they were the ones who incrementally brought Nazism home." But what would have happened if the women had used their specific "feminine" power to defy Nazism and to keep it out of their homes?

None of the women I talked to could even contemplate that they might have been able to do something against the Nazis beyond silent disapproval or small gestures of help and compassion toward others. It would not have been surprising if fear had been the reason given for not fighting openly and aggressively, since the Nazis did kill almost all the women who took part in active resistance. But these women thought that their gender alone made resistance insignificant, and they expressed this opinion not as an excuse but, rather wearily, as a still unchallenged reality. My mother, who has become a pensioner with a feminist touch, states, "I think that women are far more courageous and powerful than men, but believe me, no man could be deterred by his wife from going to war—not even if she's on her knees, begging."

Like most women of this generation, my mother (who was born in 1920) was raised in an atmosphere that discouraged women from feeling equal to men and feeling positive about themselves. A very "good," compliant daughter, she never questioned anything and grew up to become a sweet, quite strongheaded, but essentially modest and untroubled young woman. She was bright and talented but was never encouraged to develop or exercise her intellectual capacity; she therefore relied completely on her intuition and instinct, which worked like magic, and on her looks, which worked even better.

It was not so surprising, then, that my mother should have become a blissfully apolitical woman, to an almost comical degree. For her, history and politics were words that should be used exclusively by men, since they made both, and it was too bold an idea that a woman could be presumptuous enough to form her own opinion and make a contribution other than having the prettiest home on the block. She was also bored by presidents, kings, dictators, and chancellors, who seemed to her so unattractive; she didn't know their names or what they stood for, and except for Adenauer and Willy Brandt, I don't think there was anybody she could identify in all of Germany's governments. And having come from a country that for centuries had been constantly invaded and annexed by predatory foreigners, she was deeply resentful of the damage politics inevitably entailed. Politics, after all, had driven her out of her homeland.

Unfortunately, her lack of historical, political, and sociological awareness left her unable to supply detailed information about her family's history. None of the assemblage of people she described ever took on a distinctive shape; they remained fictitious, contradictory characters with endearing and amusing idiosyncrasies whose personalities changed each time my mother talked about them. Her father, Jonas Daukant, had been a professional soldier in the Russian Army (probably before and during World War I) who later moved to Latvia, where he became the supervisor of a small workshop that manufactured shoes. He read Tolstoy, looked like Clark Gable, and gambled away his wife's jewelry. Her mother, Paula, emerged as an impatient, overworked, and hotheaded *Hausfrau*, affectionate but authoritarian with her four children. Sister Luzie was beautiful and blasé; the younger sister, Anett, was sweet and lovable; and Albert, the youngest and the only boy, was a spoiled brat and their mother's darling. My mother can't remember exactly when her parents were born, how they grew up, or why they left their native Lithuania. She never asked, and regrets it to this day.

She was very good, however, at telling poignant little

stories from the perspective of a turbulent household in Nazi
Germany which sounded more like action-packed cartoons
than terrifying real-life events. I grew up with women's war
stories. Fathers had no time, and not only were their war
adventures not suitable for children but they had also buried
their memories too deep to have casual access to them.
Women had an easier time because the carnage of war was
pushed aside, clearing the way for suspenseful, life-
affirming tales that celebrated female adaptability and survival tactics under the most extreme circumstances.

One account, now enveloped in the hazy shade of forgiving nostalgia, involved the RAF. One afternoon in the
summer of 1944, the British decided to drop a few bombs
over Hamburg in the brightest of daylight, to the surprise
and horror of the already devastated population. My sister
Sylvie and my cousin Andreas were sitting in their playpen
in the garden when my mother and Aunt Trude—both
doing housewifely duties inside the house—heard the sound
of the approaching bomber. To this day, neither woman
knows how she got downstairs and into the garden in a split
second; they assume that they must have been flying. They
grabbed the babies, raised a fist to the sky, and cursed the
damned Allies.

By the end of 1944, women had grown more concerned
and more curious—and less naïve. Although it was punish-
able by death to listen to the *Feindsender* (enemy station),
many Germans, my mother and aunt included, listened
clandestinely to the BBC late at night under the cover of a
blanket. My grandmother often wondered how the two
women knew a suspicious amount about the scheduled
bombing raids. She felt she had to defend the Führer's
brilliant war strategies and firmly insisted that he had the

"wonder weapon" (the V-2 rocket) ready to go when nobody expected it, and was indignant when doubts would arise in her own house.

Another standard tale concerned the black-market adventure. My parents' version involved my mother's favorite garment, her elegant black Persian lamb coat, which my father sold—despite severe resistance from her—because he owed some money from a previous disaster in the black market. He swore that he would buy her a new coat as beautiful as the original at the next opportunity. War loosens the tongue and encourages promises that are not necessarily meant to be kept. She had to wait twenty years for that new coat, by which time fashion had changed and so had their feelings for each other. We children were always puzzled when the words "Persian lamb coat," resonant with resentment, were thrown into the middle of a heated argument between my parents.

This episode also exemplifies the many marital problems that not only were created by the psychological and economic pressures of war but were also covered up by them. The war years brought people together who wouldn't have considered each other seriously as suitable partners under less catastrophic circumstances. My parents' marriage was based on love at first sight without risking another look that would have confirmed that they had little in common other than being needy but flamboyant and dramatic personalities. But war is an unbeatable matchmaker, desperation makes people tolerant, and shared misery chains them together tighter than a band of gold. The lives of many women might have developed quite differently if the desire for harmony, security, and warmth in a troubled time had not pushed them into the arms of men, into marriage and motherhood before they could explore life and pursue self-fulfillment. Many couples married in Germany during the war just to establish this human bond, so crucial for emotional survival. Getting married meant a brief vacation from the front, a few hours or days of rushed happiness, kisses, sex, followed by the pain of separation, the nagging fear of never seeing the other alive again.

Behind every German wedding photo in the forties is a unique story that betrays the impression of sameness in fashion and mood: he in Wehrmacht uniform and she in a flower-print dress, wooden platform wedgies, and a gaudy hat ("white weddings," like my mother's, were rare). Maybe he never came back. Maybe he became a POW and suddenly reappeared after she had given up on him, almost forgotten what he looked like. Maybe she fell in love with someone else because she thought he was dead. Maybe she couldn't recognize him anymore, couldn't deal with his moods, the discouraged look on his face, the nightmares that woke him up at night, or couldn't look at the leg he dragged behind him.

The men who came home from the war often felt like uninvited visitors in the rapidly changing world of postwar Germany, which had become a society of women. They were the ones who had kept families alive and businesses profitable, who had adapted quickly to the new routines brought about by the occupying armies, who had helped to build a new nation from the rubble while the men had been gone. Moreover, many babies were born during the war and raised without fathers for the first years; it was not an atypical experience that my father had upon arriving home from Austria at the end of 1945. My sister Sylvie, who had seen him only a few times before, hid behind our mother, pointed to the man in the silly Tyrolean hat who offered her an orange, and whispered, "Mommy, when is this man leaving?" The man didn't leave, but I often felt that father and daughter could never quite smooth out the rough edges of their first meetings.

"If your father hadn't returned I think I would have had a good career in fashion or in the film business. I had great offers," she says with a proud grin, "but I will never know how I would have developed without the war. Deep down I wanted to have my freedom, explore life; but I also was confused, scared, a displaced person—and in love. When you love someone in a war you are much more dependent and insecure because of fear of losing him."

If there ever was an era that defined women as much as it was defined by them, it had to be postwar Germany, although the female home-front warriors remained strangely anonymous until today. My image of women was shaped by the women of the fifties. Underneath their assumed disguise as happy, well-adjusted, model *Hausfrauen*, responsible for unburned toast and lumpless gravy (two things my mother managed to mess up), beat the fierce hearts of unsentimental survivors who had seen it all. Their lives had been disrupted and marred by death, loss, destruction, and despair, all of which left their mark on the tough yet uncomplaining and self-deprecating widows, soldier's mothers, war brides, and street-smart "rubble women" I grew up with.

I can't say that my mother helped to build up Germany with bricks or biceps—and she wasn't too unhappy about that either—but in spite of herself, Germany had shaped her too. She had been more fortunate and privileged than most, yet she was very much part of a generation born between two world wars that wasn't raised so differently all over Europe. And although her German experience didn't precede the Nazi era, she had spent four excruciating

war years in Germany and had lived there through marriage, motherhood, middle age, and maturity.

Sadly, my mother and her generation form a silent and
nearly forgotten group of surprisingly modest and unre-
bellious caretakers without strong identities, whose hopes
and dreams were bludgeoned by the war and who never
got credit for their remarkable achievements. It may seem
somewhat contradictory that these strong women became
so conspicuously meek and conformist after the war had
forced them to be unusually brave, self-sufficient, and independent. But the *Wirtschaftswunder* seduced them with
new stoves and new furniture, and they leaped at the unusual opportunity to enjoy life and to heal their wounds in
the much-treasured uninterrupted privacy of their peaceful
and secure homes.

Once settled in their material lives, German women in
the fifties set about to construct the emotional climate with
unshakable aplomb. Unlike the men, whose experiences
never seemed to bring them closer and who couldn't progress beyond an uneasy camaraderie with each other, the
women had always felt empathy and solidarity toward one
another. They recognized the similarity of their lives and
embraced it gratefully, knowing that they needed one another's moral support and practical help. There was great
warmth and a tart sense of humor among the women in
postwar Germany and today they all cherish the memories
of a time when friendship was the center of social life. "It
was a beautiful time. I have to say that the war had made
better human beings out of the people; they helped each
other, were compassionate and less egotistical. Nobody begrudged their neighbor anything, since everybody was
happy and full of appreciation," my mother recalls. Having
coffee with neighbors several times a day while discussing

their children, dinner menus, and bargains, or gossiping about other neighbors, was a popular form of social life for the mothers and wives who didn't go to work.

Since the fifties were also a time of sexual repression that had fashioned a morality as tight as many women's permanents, there was a lot of discreet but knowing talk about marriage, infidelity, abortion—and men. The view of men and of their individual and global achievements, as projected by the women around me, was not all that positive. The war had been not only a human disaster but also a man-made failure, the women in it notwithstanding, and it confirmed neither men's superiority or intelligence in politics nor their ability to run the world peacefully. And although no one dared to contradict men's decisions openly, the women's trust in male omnipotence had been severely dented.

It seems to me that German women may have been more successful in working through the past than the men, not as a result of a conscious effort but as a by-product of their reflections on their lives. The women who were in their early twenties during the war are now grandmothers in their late sixties who only recently have begun to speak up about a time that so betrayed and shortchanged them. Unlike the men, the women feel not so much haunted as hurt by the past. They have emotionally resolved parts of the past by allowing themselves to feel the loss and face the crippling damage wrought by the war. They also have not had to maintain false identities or pretenses of heroism and glory (and since they were rarely made the focus of postwar scrutiny of the Nazi past, they are also less defensive). Some of these women have become quite emancipated and even politicized in their old age and can be found, gritty veterans that they are, actively involved in the recent German peace and environmental movements. I am left with the impres-

sion that many of these once obsequious bystanders are
more likely than their male contemporaries to protest
against social and political injustice because they are more
angry about the past. Pity is in short supply in Germany,
but it is mostly women who now show genuine sorrow for
the atrocities and killings, and although they still have difficulty accepting complicity, they have woven the bitter
lessons of war into their present lives.

My mother always felt like a victim who could never
seem to break out of the female trap. It wasn't befitting for
a woman in her thirties who lived in the fifties to violate
the traditional rules governing the unspoken deal she had
made with marriage and motherhood. She was prepared to
perfection for this thankless role because she was afraid
to complain, to demand, to criticize, and she couldn't bear
to appear ungrateful, unreasonable, difficult, or—worst of
all—selfish. To a large extent she still personified the Nazi
ideology of purity, harmony, and an idealized family life.
One of her strongest beliefs was that a woman has to sacrifice everything for her husband and children, and she
would always declare, "You children are all I have and live
for." As I have gotten older I have felt increasingly burdened
and saddened by this attitude. Her yearning for harmony
and belonging was extraordinary; she expected her husband and children to replace her lost homeland and family
and become her crutches and her identity as well. She
guarded the frail happiness of her family with passion and
perseverance because she couldn't handle the threat of dis-
pute and discordance.

I remember her as the quintessential mother, the kind
who gives and never takes, and she was quite wonderful

when we were kids. She was exuberant and full of sur-
prises—she sewed my first teddy bear and served us pud-
dings decorated with faces. We were cuddled and kissed,
and when she looked at us it was always with the radiant
smile of a proud and adoring mother. We were in love with
her. Besides being Super-Mom she was also the cook, clean-
ing woman, organizer, pedagogue, and scapegoat for everything that went wrong, and she gradually became impatient
and moody, spanked us unfairly, and even had outbursts
of anger.

When I was a teenager, she broke down once in a while,
standing by the sink and sobbing resentfully, "I'm nothing
but a servant for all of you," at which I shrugged my shoulders, gave her a quizzical look, and disappeared into my
room. Today I'm ashamed of that, but I didn't know better.
My sister and I were princesses who didn't do much house-
work, and when we did, she went over everything again
because it wasn't perfect. She began to pour her heart, her
frustration, and her energy into compulsive housecleaning
and consequently drove us all crazy. We made fun of her,
asking her condescendingly, "Mom, can't you do something
else?" But she couldn't. She had no confidence in herself
and didn't know how to pursue a career because her vague
ambitions had always been deflected, and whenever they
were revived over the years, they were stifled again by her
distaste for discipline and challenge and by my father. Although my mother did work part-time as a fashion illus-
trator for a large house when we were kids, she had to give
it up when my father learned that she would have to travel
to Paris once in a while. The idea of his beautiful wife being
outside his control *and* earning money was something my
father would not countenance without a fight. He won; she

didn't go. She was a skillful manipulator but she wasn't a fighter.

It hurts to have a mother who was nothing more than a slave whose chains were covered by fashionable accoutrements. Still believing that men were superior and women were their subordinates, she had handed herself over to my father and was absolutely dependent on him, economically and emotionally. She didn't have one pfennig to her name; instead she received a modest allowance and had to beg for every additional mark and had to justify every purchase—from a roast beef to new kitchen curtains—to my compulsively stingy father.

Her greatest talent was to eliminate the philistine odor that hung over her basically prosaic surroundings and plodding lifestyle and turn everything she touched into original and stylish miracles with very little money. On the spur of the moment she would paint the whole apartment, reupholster every chair and sofa, or do her "sew and wear" stunt. She'd toss a couple of yards of fabric on the floor, plop down next to it, drape and layer it, put a homemade pattern on it, and then start to cut with glittering eyes. During this procedure she'd put pins in her mouth, which would remain there virtually all day because she could kiss and talk without removing them. As if by magic, the outfit would be ready in the evening, for she would sew with the feverish passion of a maniac so the creation could be modeled for us kids. We would then sit on the couch, usually awestruck by such poise and elegance, and could do nothing but nod when she'd ask, "Does it look good?"

We would always watch her when she gussied herself up for a big party. She would put on her seamed nylons and some fancy high heels, and sit at her vanity in bra and girdle, painting her nails crimson with expert strokes. Then she would fetch the box with cake mascara and spit on the brush before working on her long lashes. After finishing her makeup and hair she'd slip into a strapless beaded gown, add countless accessories from boxes and drawers, and twirl around for us once before leaving in a cloud of exquisite-smelling perfume, blowing kisses at us.

Her dislike of Germany and its people's national character was never reciprocated with similar feelings by anybody she met. It was nearly impossible not to notice or like my mother, to escape her captivating charm and irresistible warmth in so relatively cold and severe an environment. She was vital and passionate, had gracious manners and a kind heart; her compliments and hugs were evenly and generously distributed among her friends—sometimes to baffled strangers as well. And she used all her charms to her advantage. She was very flirtatious—the kind of woman to whom the mailmen wanted to deliver the mail personally, in the hope of catching her in a sexy housedress, and for whom other women's husbands leaped forward to open the door. All of this didn't seem to threaten the women around her because she wasn't conceited and she always sided with them, thereby developing many lifelong friendships.

My father, in turn, was torn between raging jealousy because she was extremely popular with everybody and self-congratulatory pride because she was his. I felt the same way by the time I was sixteen because she began to be in my way—and I in hers—while I struggled for my female identity, and my ambivalence and annoyance at a mother who was really very controlling underneath all that alluring sweetness increased. She saw her daughters as symbiotic creatures that were extensions of herself and consequently her very own possessions, who weren't expected to break free from the mother bond without her permission. I particularly stirred up resentment in her because she was troubled by my rebellious side, something she had always repressed in herself. She didn't know how to integrate emotions like aggression, hate, and anger into the selfless mother-and-wife image. Instead she became dictatorial with me and watched my departure from her loving but iron grip with anguish and disappointment.

Although my mother wasn't a bad role model in terms of her self-styled looks and individual qualities—especially her invincible, upbeat spirit even in the face of adversity—I had learned early on that being female *and* being married meant pain, constriction, vulnerability, subordination, and defeat. And tears. I had seen my parents quarrel too often and my mother crying too much because she couldn't defend herself. It was a heartbreaking sight. It must have been hard for her—and disappointing as well—when she realized that I not only had not chosen her as a positive role model but saw her instead as a grim example of what happens to women if they run into the trap of giving up their identity and independence and do not have a career.

My mother never consciously discouraged her two daughters from going into the world and doing what we wanted to do, but she didn't push us either. We were a new generation and she sensed that we might be luckier than she had been. Instead, it was my father's male chauvinism that gave us confusing messages. He wanted us to work but thought that a specialized education was only for women who weren't pretty enough to do something profitable without having to work hard. He told my sister and me early on that sending us to a university was throwing money out the window because we would get married anyway.

Still, my mother envied us immensely and was very

proud because we did all the things she had secretly always wanted to do, and she admired us for our professions, our money, our freedom of choice (neither of us chose to have children). She was amazed to learn that my boyfriends cooked, went shopping, and did their own laundry, and that I made decisions based on my own judgment, not theirs. Her most heartfelt envy, however, was that we grew up in our own country and that we weren't stripped of our illusions and barred from our goals by a scarring war. "Of all the generations I can think of, mine is the most betrayed one," she says. "It is as if I was misplaced in time: whatever my aspirations and dreams were, it was always the wrong time. The war stole the best years of my life. I had to leave home when I was nineteen, I became a mother at twenty-three—finally the war was over and I was suddenly a mature woman."

Only in retrospect can I comprehend how my mother must have suffered from her uprootedness and from having virtually nobody with whom she could share these feelings. "All my life I felt like a refugee," my mother explains. "Leaving my homeland was like pushing a little bird out of his nest before he can fly. The saddest thing is that you have to leave behind your identity and what you grew up with; you can't take that with you—people, landscapes, even material objects. I'm lucky because I was able to make the transition and create a new life for myself. I used to envy my sister Luzie because she was home, but in the end I didn't regret that I didn't go back, I wouldn't have wanted to live under the Russians. But all refugees I know have this feeling of never wanting to let go of their secret dream of going back to their homeland."

I wish I had understood much earlier what it meant to her to be a refugee, forced to leave one's family, completely unprepared, and without even having the chance to say goodbye, always hoping to see them again one day (though she never did). It seems to me as if my mother gave up a large amount of her life force and self-confidence when she gave up her homeland. It hadn't been her decision to come to Germany, but it had been her free choice to stay. She learned the German language almost perfectly, but she never learned to love Germany. It wasn't her country. Why, then, had she stayed? "Because of your father" was her standard explanation.

This German husband and father took away her language, tore it up, made fun of it—and that was the worst. Sometimes she would say endearments in Lithuanian to her children or sing a little song, but her husband didn't like her "confusing them with this silly language." He never took it seriously, this little Lithuania, about which he knew absolutely nothing and which failed to interest him even after he married one of its citizens. He was quite arrogant, as if his Teutonic blood was something to be proud of. He never talked with my mother about the beautiful Baltic Sea, the white beaches that were sprinkled with amber after a big storm. He didn't want to know about her parents and siblings, her aunts and uncles. He denigrated her, minimizing everything about her country. Whenever she slept until ten in the morning, he made remarks, only half jokingly, about her "Eastern European laziness," and he accused her of upgrading her family to upper-middle-class status when he suspected that they were nothing but "little people" in an obscure small town.

"You can tell us a lot," he would say ironically, but she did. I still feel pain, thinking of how alone we left our mother in her yearnings for familiarity. She tried to make her land come alive for us (we didn't even know where the

Baltic states were until the tenth grade), describing customs
and geography, talking about her childhood and her beloved
father, who let her take ballet lessons, and we children
listened with rapt attention. But the stories were sometimes
too long for our attention span, she began to repeat them,
and when we grew impatient and interrupted her, she
would be overcome with sadness all of a sudden and would
wipe a tear from her eye. We gazed at her, touched her
hand. We didn't understand that she felt lonely and homesick. She wasn't able to save her homeland from becoming
a distant fantasy that over the years would turn into a refugee's tapestry embellished with the brilliant colors of only
happy memories of an idealized childhood. Her real tragedy
was that throughout her life there was unfinished business
she could never attend to. She was deprived of that crucial
process of tying loose ends and coming to terms with her
personal history; she couldn't reorganize and reevaluate anything that required physical confrontation with her family.
When her parents died in the late sixties and early seventies,
and her younger sister in the eighties, she had to do her
mourning while staring teary-eyed at blurry new photographs depicting old, unrecognizable people.

My mother woke up late. Only long after her daughters
were gone did she begin to come to terms with herself and
her destiny. She realized that she had indeed grown up—
in a foreign country—that her idealized childhood was gone,
that she'd probably never reunite with her remaining
brother and sister in her homeland, which was now a drab
Soviet state (she never made any attempts to visit Lithuania
or Latvia). She also realized that she didn't want to maintain
a union with a husband who was neither an understanding
friend nor a loving partner.

They separated, and freed from this tyrant she was able

to break some of her patterns and express those qualities that had lain dormant for decades. She got her first driver's license at the age of fifty-five, opened her first bank account, and did whatever came to her mind in the first apartment of her own. She learned to be more selfish and to say no, and best of all, she revived her sense of humor, which had had no chance to shine in the presence of my loquacious father. In old age she began to resemble the mother I thought I had lost in childhood—vivacious, generous, and kind. She had found the next-best thing to a homeland: a sense of self.

# 5

# *Learning What Was Never Taught*

I remember Herr Stock and Fräulein Lange without much affection. Partly because they weren't extraordinary people, partly because they failed their profession. They were my history teachers, ordinary civil servants, singled out to bring the tumultuous events of European history into perspective for a classroom of bored German schoolkids.

As it happened, Hitler and the Third Reich were the subjects under discussion when we were about fourteen years old, which is not to say that we discussed anything at all. I always thought that the decision to study the subject then was the result of a carefully calculated estimate by the school officials—as if German students were emotionally and intellectually ready to comprehend and digest the facts about Nazi Germany at exactly the age of 14.3. I learned much later that it had nothing to do with calculation; it was a matter of sequence. German history is taught chronologically, and Hitler was there when we were fourteen, whether we were ready or not.

Teaching this particular period was a thankless, though unavoidable, task. It was accompanied by sudden speech impediments, hoarse voices, uncontrollable coughs, and sweaty upper lips. A shift of mood would creep into the expansive lectures about kings and conquerers from the old ages, and once the Weimar Republic came to an end our teachers lost their proud diction.

We knew what it meant. We could feel the impending disaster. Only a few more pages in the history book, one last nervous swallowing, and then in a casual but controlled voice, maybe a touch too loud, Fräulein Lange would ask, "We are now getting to a dark chapter in German history. I'm sure you all know what I mean?"

We did, because each of us had already skimmed through the whole book countless times in search of exotic material and, naturally, had come across the man with the mustache. We knew that she was referring to the terrible time between 1933 and 1945 when Germany fell prey to a devil in brown disguise. There were fifteen pages devoted to the Third Reich, and they were filled with incredible stories about a mass movement called National Socialism which started out splendidly and ended in a catastrophe for the whole world.

And then there was an extra chapter, about three-quarters of a page long. It was titled "The Extermination of the Jews," and I had read it in my room at home many times. I always locked the door because I didn't want anybody to know what I was reading. Six million Jews were killed in concentration camps, and as I read about Auschwitz and the gas chambers a wave of feelings—fearful fascination mingled with disgust—rushed over me. But I kept quiet. What monsters must have existed then. I was glad it had all happened in the past and that the cruel Germans were gone, because, as the book pointed out, the ones responsible

were punished. I couldn't help feeling alarmed by something I couldn't put my finger on. How could so many
innocent people be murdered?

There was no explanation for my unspoken questions,
no answers in Fräulein Lange's helpless face. She seemed
embarrassed and distraught, biting her lip and looking down
at her orthopedic shoes while trying to summarize the Third
Reich in fifty minutes. That worked out to one minute for
every one million people killed in World War II . . . and
twenty-six lines for six million Jews, printed on cheap,
yellowish paper in a German history book published in
1960. An efficient time-saver, the German way.

We never read that particular chapter aloud with our
teacher as we did with so many other ones. It was the
untouchable subject, isolated and open to everyone's personal interpretation. There was a subtle, unspoken agree-
ment between teacher and student not to dig into something
that would cause discomfort on all sides. Besides, wanting
to have known more about concentration camps as a student
would have been looked upon as sick.

All things must come to an end, however, and once the
Third Reich crumbled in our classroom to the sound of
hastily turning pages, the suffocating silence was lifted.
Everybody seemed relieved, especially Fräulein Lange, who
became her jolly old self again. She had survived two world
wars, she would survive a bunch of unappreciative
teenagers.

In her late fifties in 1960, Fräulein Lange was a tiny,
wrinkled woman who matched my idea of the institutional
matron right down to her baggy skirt, steel-gray bun at the
nape of her neck, and seamed stockings. She also had a
trying predilection for Gutenberg, the inventer of movable
type, whom we got to know more intimately than Hitler.

But she did her duty, more or less. German teachers had to teach history whether they liked it or not.

The teachers of my time had all been citizens of the Third Reich and therefore participants in an epoch that only a few years after its bitter collapse had to be discussed in a neutral fashion. But what could they possibly have said about this undigested, shameful subject to a partly shocked, partly bored class of adolescents? They had to preserve their authority in order to appear credible as teachers. Yet they were never put to the test. A critical imagination and unreasonable curiosity were unwelcome traits in all the classrooms of my twelve years in school. There was no danger that a precocious student would ever corner a teacher and demand more facts about the Nazis; they could walk away unscathed. We didn't ask our parents at home about the Nazis; nor did we behave differently in school.

The truth was that teachers were not allowed to indulge in private views of the Nazi past. There were nationwide guidelines for handling this topic, including one basic rule: The Third Reich and Adolf Hitler should be condemned unequivocally, without any specific criticism or praise. In reality, however, there were basically three ways to deal with the German past: (1) to go through the chapter as fast as possible, thereby avoiding any questions and answers; (2) to condemn the past passionately in order to deflate any suspicion about personal involvement; (3) to subtly legitimate the Third Reich by pointing out that it wasn't really as bad as it seemed; after all, there were the *Autobahnen*.

But no matter what the style of prevarication, the German past was always presented as an isolated, fatal accident, and so the possibility of investigating the cause of such a disaster was, of course, eliminated. Investigating crimes reinforces guilt. If something is programmatically depicted as black and bad, one doesn't look for different shades and angles. The Third Reich was out of reach for us; it couldn't be cut down to size.

I wonder now what could have been accomplished by a teacher who had taken part in the war—as a soldier, or a Nazi, or an anti-Nazi—and who talked candidly about his personal experience. But that never happened. Instead we were showered with numbers and dates. A few million dead bodies are impossible to relate to; raw numbers don't evoke emotions. Understanding is always personal. Only stories that humanized the numbers might have reached us. Had we been allowed to draw a connection between ourselves and the lives of other people, we might have been able to identify and feel compassion. But we were not aware of how blatantly insufficiently the past was handled in school because we resented the subject as much as the teacher who was somewhat entangled in it. Teenagers generally have little interest in history lessons; we learned facts and dates in order to pass a test or get a good grade and weren't convinced that comprehension of the warp and woof of historical events made any difference to the world or anybody in particular.

Another history teacher in a new school I attended in 1962 took an activist approach, mixing pathos and drama into a highly entertaining theatrical performance. To introduce highlights of the Third Reich there was no finer actor than Herr Stock. His voice was angry, his brows furrowed, and his fist was raised when he talked about the Führer's ferocious reign. Some of the more outgoing male teachers might even mimic parts of a Hitler speech. Yet when it came time to discuss the war itself, everything went downhill. His hands stopped moving, his voice became reproach-

ful—no more victories to report. His saddest expression
was reserved for the tragic end of "Germany under National Socialist dictatorship." It was time for the untouchable
chapter again, the chapter that made Herr Stock nervously
run his hands over his bald head, clear his throat, and
mumble something about "six million Jews." It was the
chapter that made him close the book with a clap, turn his
back to the class, and announce with a palpable sigh of
relief, "Recess."

In our next history lesson that chapter was usually forgotten, and nobody followed up with any questions. Happy
to have escaped interrogation, Herr Stock turned the pages
quickly, ignoring "unpleasantries" like capitulation, denazification, and the humiliating aftermath of a defeated nation. The dark clouds were gone, the past had been left
behind, and he turned jocular and voluble again.

But Herr Stock wasn't really talking to us, he was rather
trying to convince us of something, assuming the stance of
a prosecutor. For him, the scandal wasn't the casualties of
World War II, but the resulting partition of Germany and
the malevolence of the Russians. Rage, anger, and disappointment over the lost war, always repressed or directed
at others, could be openly displayed now, disguised as righ-
teousness. "They" had stolen parts of Germany—no word
of what we stole from other countries. The Russians were
war criminals; the Germans were victims.

If I had been unexpectedly curious about Nazi Germany,
I would have received little help from my history books.
The conclusions to be drawn from a twelve-year catastrophe
packed with enough dramatic material to fill a library were
reduced to a few cryptic phrases: "The Germans showed
very little insight" and "No real feelings of contrition were

expressed." Teachers and history books were their own best examples of how to eviscerate the Nazi terror without ever really trying to come to terms with it.

But a new chapter, a new era, and a magic word—*Wirtschaftswunder*—soon revived our classroom and inspired another patriotic performance by Herr Stock. The undisputed star of German history education in the sixties was the remarkable reconstruction of postwar Germany. Now here was something an old schoolteacher could sink his teeth into. Gone were stutters and coughs. A nation of survivors had rolled up its sleeves, and Herr Stock had certainly been one of them. Here was a chance to rehabilitate Germany and put some gloss over its rotten core. Postwar Germany was a genuine communal construction, a well-made product, mass-manufactured by and for the tastes of the former citizens of the Reich. Every German with two functioning hands had taken part in rebuilding Germany, and history teachers all over the country waxed nostalgic about the united strength, the grim determination, and the close camaraderie that had helped build up Germany brick by brick.

We schoolchildren couldn't have cared less about these achievements. We were all born under occupation; the postwar years were ours too and the memories of ruins and poverty were just as indelible—if not as traumatic—as they had been for our parents. But in his enthusiasm he overlooked the fact that his words were falling on deaf ears: we didn't like Herr Stock; nor did we trust or admire him. In all this excitement about the "economic miracle," another, even greater miracle was conveniently left unexplained. On page 219 of my history book, Germany was described as a nation living happily under National Socialism and a seemingly accepted Führer without any visible crisis of conscience. Yet only fourteen pages later the same *Volk* is depicted in the midst of an entirely different world, miraculously denazified and retrained, its murderous past neatly tucked away behind a tattered but nevertheless impenetrable veil of forgetfulness.

How did they do it? The existing Federal Republic of Germany is only one state away from the Nazi Reich. Where did they unload the brown ballast? The role change from obedient Nazi citizen to obedient *Bundes* citizen went too smoothly from *"Sieg Heil!"* to democracy, and from marching brown uniforms to marching gray flannel suits. Where was the genuine substance which had initially constituted the basic foundation and ideology of the Third Reich? Could it still be there, hidden, repressed, put on ice?

Such questions were never asked, or encouraged. The schoolteachers that I encountered were a uniformly intimidating group of people (with one glorious exception): older men and women who demanded respect, order, and obedience. They were always curbing my curiosity with the clobbering logic of people who get paid for controlling outbursts of independent thinking. Their assessment of my character in report cards read: "She talks too much and could accomplish more if she would be more diligent."

Even though prohibited when I went to school, corporal punishment in many forms was still practiced with parental support, and my own classroom recollections are thick with thin-lipped, hawk-eyed, bespectacled men and women with mercilessly firm hands ready to take up the switch.

I always felt powerless toward teachers, and all of these emotions crystallized in 1983, when I was preparing to interview one of them. I couldn't help feeling a little triumphant. I was asking the questions now because I had discovered a slight spot on their white vests, something I couldn't see clearly when I was young and under their control. Now I had the power to make them nervous. My victory over German authority seemed complete. A school-girl's revenge?

But that wasn't all. I had a genuine interest in finding out how teachers in Germany feel today about their past failures. Had they found new ways to justify their damaging elisions, euphemisms, and omissions? More than any other age group, my generation was in desperate need not only of historical education but also of some form of emotional assistance from the adults who were linked to that not so distant yet unspeakable past.

In a way, I was looking for Herr Stock. But teachers as mediocre as he and Fräulein Lange had little to contribute to the kind of discussion I had in mind: I wanted the perspective of a teacher who had at least attempted to come to grips with his past. I was lucky to find one in Cäsar Hagener, a seventy-six-year-old former teacher and history professor. Hagener lives with his wife in a cozy, old-fashioned house with a garden in a suburb of Hamburg, in a quiet, safe neighborhood with lots of trees, many dachshunds, and little activity. He owns the type of one-family house, surrounded by a fence, that was commonly built in the thirties. A German house must have a fence. A house without a fence is disorderly, like a coat with a missing button.

Cäsar Hagener exuded integrity and an appealing friendliness—yet I found it impossible to forget that he had also been a teacher in the Third Reich. Hitler had envisioned a training program that would make every German youth "resilient as leather, fast as a weasel, and hard as Krupp steel." He believed that "too much education spoils the youth." (Not surprisingly, after a few years of dictatorship

30 percent of the university professors, including Jews, had left the country.)

In 1933, Cäsar Hagener was a teacher of pedagogy and history at a liberal school in Hamburg, and when he heard that Hitler was appointed Reichs Chancellor he happened to be studying *Das Kapital* together with some left-wing colleagues. "My friend said to me, 'It'll be over in no time. When you and I write a history book in twenty years, the Nazis will only be a footnote.' "

Even a skillful dictator like Hitler couldn't turn a country upside down overnight, and school life changed slowly under the Nazis. "But after 1934, the Nazis began to investigate the teachers' adaptation to the new order. Some were fired, and some were retrained in special camps. We had, of course, some 'overnight' Nazis who were strutting around in uniform, which didn't impress the students, who were quite critical. Later, in 1937, the young teachers were told to join the Nazi Party or else, so I joined the Party. Still, the first years of National Socialism were almost bearable."

However, at least once a week, teachers and students had to muster for the raising of the swastika flag and the singing of the "Horst-Wessel-Lied" or other Nazi songs. The Führer's speeches were required listening on the popular *Volksempfänger* for teachers and older students, while the nazified text in the new schoolbooks read like this: "If a mental patient costs 4 Reichsmarks a day in maintenance, a cripple 5.50, and a criminal 3.50, and about 50,000 of these people are in our institutions, how much does it cost our state at a daily rate of 4 Reichsmarks—and how many marriage loans of 1,000 Reichsmarks per couple could have been given out instead?"

The new features of Nazi education like race hygiene and heredity theory were given different degrees of importance in different schools. Hagener prepared himself: "I made sure to get a class with school beginners because children of that age weren't taught history or any of that Nazi nonsense. Besides, as a teacher, you were pretty much independent in your classroom and could make your own decision about what to say and what to skip. There were ways of getting around the obnoxious Nazi ideology."

The first public action by the Nazis right after January 1933 was to purge public and school libraries of "Jewish and un-German elements," leaving empty spaces on the shelves, since new "literature" wasn't written yet and new schoolbooks, adapted to the Nazis' standards, weren't printed until 1936. That same year they initiated compulsory membership in the Hitler Youth, starting at the age of ten with boys organized into Jungvolk and Hitler Jungen and girls and young women into the Bund Deutscher Mädel (League of German Girls). What the Reich of the future needed were fearless, proud men of steel and yielding, fertile women—preferably blond—not effete intellectuals.

"The children can't be blamed for having been enthusiastic members of the Hitler Youth," Cäsar Hagener points out. "They grew up with that ideology and couldn't be expected to protect themselves from National Socialism; to do so, children would have had to be unaffected by all outside influences. It was their world, and the Hitler Youth programs were very attractive, with sports, contests, and decorations. It was possible for the son of a Communist or a Social Democrat to become a highly decorated Hitler Youth leader. I accuse the teachers who didn't perceive what was going on, and who taught Nazi ideology and glorified war, of having failed their profession."

In the last years of the war there was not much academic activity in Germany. The Nazi state was concerned with other problems besides education. Many schools were destroyed by bombs and virtually all Germans between fifteen and sixty years of age—Cäsar Hagener was drafted in 1940—were mobilized for the *Endkampf* (the final struggle) by the end of 1944. Hunger, death, and the will to survive prevailed over culture and education. Who needs to know algebra when the world is falling apart?

In 1945 denazification fever broke out in the defeated nation and reversed the roles of master and servant. For over a decade the country had been straining to purge itself of "un-German elements," and now the occupying powers were trying to purge it of all Nazi elements. Yet their efforts only exposed the unfeasibility of such a gargantuan task, since it involved much more than just the Nazi Party and the SS. Twelve years under the swastika had produced all kinds of "literature," art, music, film—indeed, a whole society had to be taken apart and its guiding principles destroyed. Naturally, reforming the educational system was a high priority, and millions of schoolbooks were thrown out, but some had to be preserved. The specially assigned Allied education officers decided which schoolbooks could still be used (after tearing out a Nazi-contaminated page or censoring a suspicious chapter or two). The approved books were stamped, and were circulated until new ones could be printed, which wasn't until the early fifties.

"The British, our occupiers, did everything wrong, because nothing could be worked out intellectually. They came over here with certain expectations and this incredibly bad image of the enemy, and they were very surprised to find their task not as easy as they had thought. They tried to control the situation by being very strict."

Reforming the faculty was even more problematic, since many teachers had been forced to join the Nazi Party and it wasn't always easy to tell who was a "real" Nazi and who wasn't. As a rule of thumb, those who appeared to have cooperated unwillingly were permitted to continue teaching, younger teachers who had been educated under the Nazi regime were retrained in special seminars, while those who had been active supporters were barred from teaching for as long as two years.

Cäsar Hagener still gets angry over how easily former colleagues were rehired. "After 1945, nobody seemed to remember what a Nazi was, and people who I knew were definitely Nazis by nature landed on top again. I was one of a group of young teachers who protested violently against this tendency—and I felt like a McCarthy witch-hunter. I saw these people as criminals who did a lot of harm to us teachers."

Still, the main consideration was that teachers were badly needed. The war had wiped out a whole generation of young men, and keeping professionals from their profession in Germany after 1945 was as uneconomical as it was impractical: what was left was what Germany's children got. It's safe to say that by 1950 almost all teachers were back in schools and universities regardless of their past.

In the years immediately following the war, the few schools that were not badly damaged were overcrowded with children of all ages and several grades gathered together in one room. There was cardboard in place of windows, and opening umbrellas inside the school on rainy days was as natural as being sent home for a "cold-weather holiday" because there was no heat. The teacher had to be a good-humored ringmaster, innovative and full of stories; because of the book shortage, he had to know his lessons by heart. The students also needed good memories, because there wasn't any paper. Arithmetic and grammar assignments were often written down on the margins of newspapers.

It might have been the only time in Germany when school lessons were extemporaneous, personal, and an accurate reflection of real life. School was suddenly a popular place where humanity prevailed over theory. Teachers were not merely authority figures but people who had been harmed by the war just like the students and their families, and much of the time was spent discussing how to steal potatoes and coal and other survival tactics, which were more pressing than Pythagoras.

How did a teacher in those years explain history while it was happening? The change from "Nazis are good" to "Nazis are bad" must have been a confusing experience for the uprooted, disillusioned children of the Third Reich. Children weren't denazified. They had to adapt to "democracy" without shedding a brown skin. All the values they had learned to defend so passionately crumbled before their eyes and the reality they once trusted was rearranged silently, without their consent. The glorious, thunderous Third Reich was a gyp. The Jews weren't "*Volks* enemy number one" anymore. And as for the Führer, he wasn't a superhuman hero, but a vicious little coward, a maniac who wanted to exterminate a whole people and almost succeeded. What irreparable mistrust must have become lodged in the minds of all these young Germans whose youth was trampled flat by goose-stepping jackboots.

But teachers didn't explain history at all. "I'm afraid to say that it didn't occur to the students to bring up Adolf in any form. We had all survived and dealt mostly with the effects of the war in a practical sense. I tried to do nice, positive things with the children, who had it bad enough as it was," Cäsar Hagener explains, and adds, almost surprised, "It is amazing how extremely apolitical we were.

Any reflection was impossible under the circumstances, because everything was defined in terms of the struggle of daily life, which had a dynamic all by itself."

He also knows why the adolescents of the fifties and sixties were as uninquisitive as their teachers and parents were silent. "There was strong resentment toward the grown-ups. The teenagers had a fine sense for the things that didn't quite fit together with the Nazis. I didn't have any luck with my own three sons; they frustrated my desire to talk about the past by calling it lecturing, so I ended up talking about it mostly in foreign countries, where the people seemed to be more interested in it."

Things have changed radically during the last twenty years. There has been a small revolution in the German classroom. While teachers after the war were much younger and more outspoken than their predecessors, students became rebellious and undisciplined.

Cäsar Hagener remembers his school days. "My own generation and my students lived in a very strict and conformist structure which existed much earlier than 1933. Sure, there were provocative and rebellious personalities, but this phenomenon of developing an independent mind is new. Today it wouldn't be possible to stand in front of a class in uniform and in all seriousness talk about racial theory. The students would die laughing."

German students today often know more facts about the Third Reich than both their parents and the immediate postwar generation, and are not afraid to ask questions. Yet their interest in Nazism is strictly intellectual, and they generally succeed in remaining emotionally detached. They don't know yet that they can't escape the past. Tragically, almost all of Cäsar Hagener's contemporaries have managed to escape their Nazi past. In his opinion: "You can't put a whole nation on the couch. I find my own contemporaries just plain terrible and I don't have much contact with many old friends anymore. In their eyes I'm too critical, a guy who fouls his own nest and who can't see the good sides of the Nazi era—which infuriates and bores me at the same time. They reject the radical examination of the past. But it's necessary, since we know better than most that terrible things can and did happen."

# 6

## *Soldiers All Look Alike*

I never liked soldiers. Never liked to look at them, talk to them, or be too close to them, probably due to a deep-rooted suspicion that they might start a war any minute. Being a German means having a problem with uniforms, *all* uniforms, and my strong aversion was established at an early age.

Perhaps my attitude toward uniforms might have been different if I had been the lucky recipient of treasures like chewing gum and chocolate bars from the hands of the liberating Americans, something that actually happened to some of my older friends who didn't grow up in the British zone. (Tommies seem to have been more conservative and stingy, since there's no evidence for their generosity.)

As I was growing up, there were three basic kinds of uniforms. Those of the British were mildly interesting and not particularly alarming. The police, still in their majestic black-and-silver pre-World War II getup, were far more

intimidating. Later, in 1956, we were introduced to the
brand-new and very benign light-gray uniforms of the
newly formed Bundeswehr (German Army), for which I
had only contempt as a teenager; they made the freshly drafted, eager-faced eighteen-year-old boys look like
dressed-up toy soldiers. (I am certain that the German uniform designers had strict orders to move light-years away
from anything that might resemble the notorious Nazi cou-
ture in cut and color.)

My father occasionally made acerbic and derogatory remarks about the mentality of people who wear uniforms,
including Nazis, policemen, and even mailmen. Uniforms
meant war, and nothing good could be expected from people
whose clothes were synonymous with evil and destruction;
I couldn't imagine that I'd ever associate soldiers with peace.

Uniforms are purposeful working clothes with a psychological undercurrent: they bestow identity, power, and a
sense of camaraderie to people who can't find it elsewhere.
Women love them; they flatter the male ego, disguise the
flawed body, and make up for any absence of taste that
might be visible in civilian clothes. They take away individuality, and with it the sense of personal responsibility:
he who slips into a uniform hands over his conscience and
suppresses his questions. The uniformity of the clothes encourages conformity of the mind. Soldiers all look alike,
dead or alive.

Pondering the visible totems of war begs the question:
Which came first? the uniform or obedience? the gun or
the desire to kill? Marching itself can be a form of expression. The most spectacular marching extravaganzas of all
time were staged and documented by the Nazis, to a point
where the art of marching is now considered a German

trademark, often copied but never surpassed. That unmistakable step, made with breathtaking precision: a picture of perfectly beautiful horror.

To be a German means constantly having to deal with war. After so many years it is still an integral part of the national conscience, woven into all aspects of our life. The two world wars have defined the lives of six consecutive generations—mine being the fifth. My German great-great-grandparents died after World War I; my great-grandparents died in 1946, over the age of ninety; my grandparents also lived through both world wars. My father spent his early childhood in World War I and his adulthood in World War II. When I think of my ancestors, I realize that mine is the first German generation of the twentieth century that has grown to a relatively mature age without actually having been involved in a war. Sometimes it feels almost unnatural.

In first grade I was introduced to one of those endlessly long German jawbreakers even a native has trouble pronouncing, and while I never really understood its meaning, it connected two things I did know about: war and money. *Kriegsgräbergroschen* (war-graves dimes) were the twenty pfennigs my teacher collected once a year, throughout the early fifties, for a faceless group of soldiers we were told lay buried in cemeteries everywhere, killed in the terrible war.

Many years later I would see what war cemeteries looked like: neatly arranged graves with endless rows of crosses, one like the other. The monotony of war had found its profoundest expression in war cemeteries, where anonymous skeletons were grouped under two common denominators, one group bearing the years 1939 to 1945, and a much smaller one, the years 1914 to 1918.

The teacher didn't really say how and why these millions
of brave men died, although we all knew that there was a
big war not too long ago. But she tried to explain what the
money was for while we sat quietly in the classroom, assuming an air of piety we couldn't feel but knew was expected from us. The dimes were for the care of the countless
graves of soldiers who had been buried unknown or far
away from home. Of course, the money came from our
parents; we were only the bearers, once again a link between
guilt and innocence. "They were fighting for all of us," said
Fräulein Wybkema with deep gratitude. For me too?

Meanwhile, the grown-ups had their own project to attend to. In one of the government's clumsy attempts to
institutionalize the remembrance of the wars and their victims, and to demonstrate that Germans are capable of sorrow and pity, a Sunday in November was declared a "Day
of National Mourning." It was hard to tell whether the
nation was mourning or being mourned. The whole affair
was yet another example of heartless German bureaucracy:
organized tears and sadness by decree. Statesmen with
stony cemetery faces, dressed in black, carried stiff laurel
wreaths to various monuments and set the tone for the
gloomy event with carefully selected words of warning. The
radio played Bach and Beethoven all day, and the flags were
lowered to half-staff. Well, let's all be repentant and sorry
today so that we can be all the happier and free of guilt
tomorrow.

Another way the Germans tried to cope with pain and
suffering was to erect war monuments everywhere while
rebuilding the country at that famous rapid pace. Mourning
longs for shiny marble, it seems, but the need to honor
stones still feels cold to me. I never understood the rationale
behind these depressing monoliths and ponderous statues.

Do we have to denounce war with symbols of war? Is it worth dying just to have your name chiseled into stone?

In the center of Hamburg is a particularly impressive monument which has been a source of controversy ever since it was erected right after the war: an enormous concrete oblong relief with nasty-looking Nazi soldiers, guns over their shoulders, helmets on their heads, and the inscription "Many sons of the city gave their lives for you" under their jackboots. As long as I can remember, this atrocious eyesore has been splashed with paint and marked with various antiwar slogans, while the city spends a fortune to have it cleaned up periodically—to no avail.

"Unbelievable, a shame," the older citizens still complain when they pass by. "A scandal," fume the younger people, "to keep such disgusting Nazi art in the middle of the city." It would be interesting to see how all the German war memorials would look if they hadn't been commissioned by government employees and carried out by artless artists, but were the work of survivors or of relatives and friends of the victims of war.

Who decides who is worthy of memorials, celebration, and recognition and who qualifies for the edification of posterity? The German state is very choosy and ungenerous in its selection of an "appropriate" group of people. Certified heroes seem to be the most deserving because they died in a noble way, even in an ignoble war; ordinary people just don't have enough stature, regardless of what they did or what was done to them. Because there were so few acts of opposition of heroic proportions, the few "official" fighters of the Nazi regime heroic enough to get top billing on walls, monuments, and street signs, as well as in museums and schoolbooks, are usually those who were involved in the Hitler assassination attempt and in the anti-Nazi White

Rose student movement. The Jewish victims are mostly honored in the places where they were once sent to die— former concentration camps which have been transformed into memorials. Few, however, have been left intact and these are not easily accessible without substantial traveling.

The world honors selectively. "Heroes" and "victims" are by no means universal labels; they are sharply divided into "ours" and "theirs," for one nation's hero is another's enemy. It is not permissible to graciously mourn the losses of a foreign nation even if the soldiers died on the same battlefield. Surely, for all the torrent of blood, unclassified blood, that soaked the soil of Europe and elsewhere, it should be an honor to erect common memorials across all borders and oceans. Why shouldn't we be reminded of the incomprehensible losses suffered by the Russian people at the hands of the attacking Germans—maybe right in the middle of Frankfurt or Heidelberg? What is so absurd about a memorial honoring the Polish and Czech populations and apologizing for the brutal slaughter of their people? Around the world, monuments might be exchanged between countries that had once fought against each other: America, Russia, Spain, Japan, Israel, Vietnam, China, Korea, France, Ireland, Afghanistan . . . It might enhance our awareness of other people's suffering and help us to understand that wars are fought by people, not by countries. "Their" wars are our wars too.

There is also a case for erecting several different kinds of memorials. To my knowledge, no memorial yet exists for the displaced persons who were kept in camps where they often died, nor is there one for the victims of euthanasia or the enormous groups of forced-labor workers who were recruited from the occupied countries. Where are all the memorials for the Jews that one can actually see? Or those for the mothers and widows and nurses of the soldiers, women without whose courage and tenacity Germany could never have been rebuilt in so short a time? And how about for the children of war, dead or alive, whose joyless childhoods were punctuated by bombs and corpses, instead of teddy bears and kindergarten?

Finally, it might be a useful exercise to single out some of the perpetrators and the powerful, less noble-spirited groups who could have saved lives but failed to do so. Where are the reminders in many churches all over Germany to inform the churchgoers that in the darkest hours of Nazi terror those holy places usually offered no protection or comfort for the troubled and the persecuted? (It should be pointed out, however, that there were also several pastors and bishops who repudiated the Nazis and helped save many lives.)

Why not take one of the sculptures that usually stand by the entrances of concentration camps and place it where IG-Farben's building once stood, as a reminder that this company was partly built on the sweat and blood of concentration-camp prisoners before they were sent to the gas chambers? Or how about a little marble plate in the Krupp, AEG, Flick, and Thyssen factories to remind the indifferent employees that one can be a ruthless supporter of a criminal regime and still keep one's seat in the front row without severe repercussions. There could also be a little plaque in the prosperous Mengele factory commemorating the family's infamous son, Josef, the sadistic Auschwitz doctor, as a reminder that a wealthy, prominent family that protects a war criminal for some forty years can still do a thriving business internationally without fear of a major boycott.

Public interpretation of the past can often be a delicate task, on either side of the "Iron Curtain." The East German government, for example, is very proud of the fact that it fought fascism more aggressively and persecuted Nazi criminals more relentlessly than West Germany after the partition in 1945, and claims its half of the nation to be Nazi-free. One section of East Germany's Museum for the History of the German People is reserved for the Holocaust, where bunk beds, clothes, soup bowls, and one of those wooden "horses" onto which prisoners were tied and beaten to a pulp are on display behind glass. Yet here too there are limits, and one corner is concealed by dark curtains and a sign warns that behind them is an exhibit so shocking it should be viewed only at one's own risk. At the push of a button, the curtains open to display such gruesome objects as a lampshade made of human skin.

The sight of soldiers still frightens me, even though the next great war isn't likely to be fought by men on a battle-field. Where are the soldiers of peace? There once was a time, in 1944–45, when the sight of certain uniforms was greeted with enthusiasm all over Europe. The uniformed liberators freed Europe from their uniformed oppressors. Weapons forced Germany to make peace. Since then, weapons have protected the peace on earth. Soldiers are still the implements of war, and not much more than that. Are they sanctioned killers or just patriots, dedicated professionals, and drafted citizens who obey the call of duty? Their individual opinions, religions, and philosophies are unimportant; the government decides who the enemy is, without asking for its soldiers' approval or consent.

What would they all be without their soldiers—the dangerous dictators and egotistical statesmen? Their immortality was built on the deaths of countless anonymous fighters who believed in their country. Politicians dream about power and glory, but other men die for these dreams while they live in isolated luxury, walk on red carpets, shake hands with a widow or two, and wipe away a false tear.

To get their soldiers into the right fighting spirit, the politicians appeal to their emotions through propaganda. First, a war gets glamorized. It's made to look like an exciting adventure. In these "war games" a soldier can prove his manhood by getting a chance to flirt with danger and death. Then, a hateful image of the enemy must be produced because a successful war needs a convincing cause. How else will the soldiers be motivated to overrun foreign countries and destroy the lives of people whose language they don't even speak, whose culture and character they don't know at all? How else does one justify shooting strange men, women, and children, torturing them, raping them, burning down their homes, bombing their cities, and extinguishing their existence?

Such mutilation of feelings and bodies doesn't go unrewarded. The military is an organization whose members get a medal pinned to their green, khaki, navy-blue, or field-gray chests for killing and winning. These peculiar pieces of decoration are made of metal and meaningful colored stripes, designed to evoke respect, admiration, and sometimes envy in the onlooker, who is always a man. They are coveted prizes, neatly divided into various classes depending on the degree of bravery and luck, cherished and kept in little boxes for the next generation of sons to behold in awe. (And it will only be the emotional wives, mothers, and daughters who, in their typical lack of appreciation for wars, will question the value of all the medals in the world when a man has lost his leg and his spirit.)

The singular purpose of war is to win it. The loss as a result of war is tragic, but the loss as a result of a lost war is unbearable. If a war is won, its soldiers are heroes, dead or alive. If it is lost, they are either forgotten or shunned as the reminders of defeat. The applause of the nation belongs to the victors; the losers are left with their nightmares.

This has been particularly true for the German Wehrmacht soldiers of World War II and, at least in the beginning, for the Vietnam vets. Both came to feel anger and disappointment once they realized that the wars they had embarked on with such patriotic fervor turned out to be a fatal ignominy for their nations. In the end, an attempt was made to rehabilitate the Vietnam vets, but German soldiers are forever held in contempt by association. There was an enormous difference between the American knights in uniform returning from a noble cause "over there" after World War II and the defeated Wehrmacht soldiers dragging themselves home to their demolished country as they and other Germans confronted the shameful crimes that had been committed in their name. However, there were plenty of ordinary servicemen who fought with bravery and in good faith for their fatherland and not for Hitler, not necessarily knowing that the regime they had sworn an oath to was a criminal organization, and who tried to do their jobs at the front as correctly and fairly (if that's possible in a war) as any soldier can.

Given the fundamental principles of war, then, the Wehrmacht soldiers deserve their medals as much (or as little) as anyone else. When it comes to fulfillment of duty there's no difference: all soldiers follow orders and risk their lives; they all long to go home and be with family and friends; and they all kill innocent people. They all fear death, feel pain, and bleed like everyone else, and the tears that are shed for them are salty everywhere. The only difference is in their uniforms. The soldiers of Nazi Germany can never wear their medals in public without arousing protest; I think few feel the desire. Their reward for having believed in a deceitful dictator lies rusting among boxes of junk in dark basements. In addition, they are not very successful at bringing their war experiences alive at home; the wife can't bear to hear about it anymore, the children are unimpressed and say, "Daddy, spare us with your battle adventures." Only when the disgraced warriors get together with their war buddies can they find people who understand and can share the memories.

Germans don't do their true mourning publicly; they can't expect too much sympathy from the rest of the world for their twenty million casualties in World War II. If you are a Nazi-generation German, after all, whatever pain you might suffer is deemed your own fault. Where do you hide the pain? Behind some strangely cold and disconnected act of pretentious penitence, like that "Day of National Mourning."

My abomination for Wehrmacht soldiers was dented for the first time a few years ago while I was watching a compilation of rare footage about the liberation of Paris. The documentary showed daily life in Paris under the German occupation, complete with swastikas and strolling SS men, apparently without a care in the world. I slumped back in my seat, embarrassed as usual to be part of this nation, hoping that nobody would find out after the screening. Even the Führer came by for a visit, and the wildly incongruous image of tourist Hitler smiling and waving into his chroniclers' camera at the foot of the Eiffel Tower was perversely funny.

This assumed superiority of petty war employees gone wild in "*tout Paris*" intensified my abhorrence for Germans in general, and I waited impatiently (probably like the rest of the French) for a mighty force to crash down and destroy these predatory invaders.

Half an hour later, however, I began to feel less antagonistic. Paris was liberated, and I saw the confused faces of the young German soldiers whose eyes were begging for their lives. The tables had turned, and now *they* were the victims. The hate of the Parisians erupted and vented itself on men who had done what was asked of them, incapable of doubt. The Nazi soldiers were now brutally beaten and humiliated, just as they had done so often to others. Five civilians grabbed a German and angrily ripped the eagle off his jacket. A troop of armed French resistance fighters found several panic-stricken German soldiers in a hideout and violently drove them out, hands over their heads.

"They deserve to die," I thought, but my satisfaction with this vengeful retaliation dissipated at the sight of the terror on these young soldiers' faces. I had an impermissible emotion: I felt compassion for them. Not because they were guiltless, but because they were human. Regardless of who is winning or losing the battle of the moment, everybody is a prisoner of war. The war *is* the prison, and the greatest illusion is a victorious war. Wars are always lost, their damage irreparable. War wounds everybody. When will the idea of war finally be destroyed and stripped of the nobility and honor that is attached to it?

I always liked cemeteries, felt drawn to them because they were legitimate places for peaceful silence. After I turned thirty, however, I suddenly felt strangely mournful about the dead who had been killed in wars. Yet how was I supposed to release my sadness? How does one cry collectively for millions of dead souls one never knew? It was very unconscious at first, and I didn't realize immediately what I was searching for on my long walks through cemeteries.

I would go there with the same longing I felt going down to the harbor in Hamburg: to watch the ships passing by, and to bid farewell to imaginary passengers, strangers who disappeared from my sight forever, leaving me behind, feeling excluded and slightly forlorn. The ships and the cemetery were metaphors for lost opportunities.

Once I sat on a bench in a cemetery in front of an ugly, dark gravestone and the buried bones of an unknown Willi or Hans and wept over the inscription: "Born 1929—Died 1944." At least he had a gravestone, which is more than can be said of untold numbers of Jews. They disappeared from the face of the earth, without a stone or a flower to remember them by. I would have wanted to cry at a Jewish grave, but there were none to be found among the common graveyards. I had to find them within myself.

# 7

# *Excuse Me, Are You Jewish?*

If first impressions are crucial, my relationship with Jews got off to a heart-wrenching, alienating start. Jews were introduced to me dead: as enormous piles of skin and bones, twisted limbs and distorted faces, waiting to be tossed into carts bound for the crematory; as layers of bodies which had toppled over into long, freshly dug trenches after the bullets had hit the backs of their necks; as a cloud of smoke ascending from a brick chimney in Auschwitz. I met them through old newsreels in the sixties—wordless, grainy celluloid figures caught in a deadly pantomime, without a trace of color or a right to live. Marked with a star and invariably forced to gather in long, tight rows, they were always on their way to be killed.

But if they hadn't been sent to the gas chambers, I might have made friends with flesh-and-blood Jews without these haunting images slamming a wall of shame and guilt between us. I could have grown up with Jewish kids who were just ordinary brats like me, and we would have related without animosity because this black cloud of persecution would not have hung over them. And I wouldn't have had to deal with the fact that it was my people who had invented and carried out the efficient, cold-blooded genocide that killed most of them.

Since Jews were an abstract race for me, they remained mythological for a very long time. Even the word "Jew," the embodiment of shame and ignominy, couldn't be formed by German lips; it was as extirpated from any German's vocabulary as were the people themselves from most of our lives after the war. The terrible truth is that Hitler's murderous task, euphemistically called "the final solution of the Jewish question," was completed successfully. When I was born, Germany was indeed *Judenrein* (free of Jews), not just numerically but also in the conscience of the Germans. They killed the Jews twice—first their bodies, then their souls.

That the Jews were never allowed to resurrect in spirit is a special act of crime against humanity, and only a people who could not mourn or feel loss could have committed it. And yet, although the Jews' physical presence was extinguished after the doors of the gas chambers closed, their nonexistence itself became imperishable like a phantom that could never be located, encircled, or confronted. The "unmentionable ones" became permanent ghosts who kept haunting their murderers—murderers who had become as silent as their victims.

A darkly comical example of why indeed it wasn't easy to meet a Jew in Germany was provided by one of my closest Jewish friends in America. In 1955, he was a sixteen-year-old exchange student sent by the American Field Service to spend three months with a German family in Hannover. This family had all the earmarks of a classic

postwar German sitcom. Tante Erika, the fat and jolly pro-
prietress of the one-family house, was an indomitable
widow whose husband had been killed in World War II;
his nicely framed photograph in Wehrmacht uniform graced
the piano in the dining room. She reigned over the family,
as well as the butcher shop and the slaughterhouse, both
of which were located in the building. Heinz and Klaus,
her two blond, Aryan-looking sons, possessed the new postwar haughtiness of youngsters, went to the *Gymnasium*, and
looked down on their proletarian mother's thriving pork-
chop-and-oxtails business in spite of the big diesel Mercedes
in the garage.

The American teenager was shown around, dragged to
the Wagner Festival in Bayreuth to feast on Valkyries (he
fell asleep), and fed lots of knockwurst and cold cuts for
supper and delicious homemade plum torte for Sunday
breakfast. They all got along famously and Tante Erika was
sobbing when she said goodbye to the adorable Ami. There
was just one little thing. He never told the family that he
was Jewish. "Why not?" I wanted to know. "I was afraid,"
he said. "What did you think they would do to you?" I
asked. "I don't know," he answered, "but don't forget that
it was then only ten years after they had sent my people to
the gas chambers."

So I couldn't even say for sure when and if I had first
met a Jew before I came to America. Maybe it was in Italy,
England, Denmark, or Holland? Maybe the ones I had met
were afraid to tell me, a descendant of their people's persecutors, who they were. Nobody introduced himself with
the announcement "Hello, I'm Jewish," not in Germany
and not in other European countries I traveled in when I
was twenty. I would have needed such an introduction.

I found out later that my parents did have some Jewish

friends, who visited for parties and dinners when I was little, but they were never pointed out to me. I didn't grow up with anti-Semitic remarks, although some might say that silence is itself a form of slander. My father often recounted that he had met many Eastern European Jews in Berlin during the war and was quite fond of "typical Jewish" humor. That was all I picked up: that Jews are witty. Apart from that, I could have been surrounded by Cohns and Rosenbergs, Bernsteins and Finks, with faces and characteristics commonly associated with Jews, and it wouldn't have meant a thing to me. Not even "chutzpah," a word that was used liberally and with grudging respect by my father to describe aspects of my personality, which I took as a backhanded compliment, rang a bell. It was just a funny word.

But my innocent oblivion wasn't restricted to the Jews. I knew as little when I met a Jew for the first time as I knew if and when I met one of their German killers. Maybe it was Doerthe Biesterfeld, a pretty, dark girl with a well-groomed ponytail I went to elementary school with, whose parents had to wear a yellow star but miraculously survived, and maybe it was Herr Schmidt from Rauchstrasse Nr. 17, a nice, charming fellow, who had to wear the uniform that gave him license to kill.

If a people is destroyed physically and spiritually, all you're left with are selected scraps and sketchy ideas that betray the richness and uniqueness of individual lives. Deep down I was fascinated by Jews and wanted to know about them. But since nobody would talk, I had to collect my images exclusively from TV films and photos (the latter usually found in the obligatory coffee-table book about the terrible Third Reich, which gathered dust on every family's shelf).

For me the strangest-looking Jews were the Orthodox ones, and I studied their dignified, old-fashioned appearance with great attention. I didn't care much about religion (both of my parents, one Catholic, one Protestant, had abandoned the teachings of the Church as adults) and didn't see a connection between faith and clothes, except that for my confirmation I was forced to wear an unflattering dark dress, as if God would care. One photograph I saw, of a rabbi standing next to an SS officer, was chilling and also fateful in its traumatic collision between brutality and faith—two worlds, two enigmas, two stark and striking outfits that were the antithesis of each other and yet were forever linked symbolically by death. I realized that Germans and Jews were a little like Siamese twins; you couldn't look at one without seeing the other.

When Jews were shown standing together in groups, I was able to distinguish some of the faces. Why were these people so feared that their existence had to be crushed, that everything that was part of them had to be burned, shattered, and mutilated? What magical power did they possess that made them so dangerous that they had to be put behind barbed wire? Unconsciously searching for a sign in their appearance that would impart just a hint of what the Germans found so hateful and so fearful, I concluded that, on the whole, they looked better than the Germans—the lack of uniforms alone (a big advantage) might have accounted for my impression. The women, most of whom had beautiful curly hair, and the men, in their long coats and tweed caps, bore no resemblance to the celebrated Nordic, Nazi ideal. They had soulful eyes and solid, human faces devoid of the inherently Teutonic arrogance and vanity.

They didn't all have those enormous hook noses, protruding eyes, huge lower lips that hung down to their chins, fat bellies and seedy smiles, the way they were depicted as caricatures in Hitler's Jew-baiting, filthy newspaper, *Der Stürmer*, which I had once seen in facsimile in a history book. Standing there, boxes and suitcases in their hands, these Jews did not corroborate *Der Stürmer*'s contention that they were avaricious cutthroats and innately vile individuals. They looked like forlorn people who had a dark premonition that this might be a trip without a return.

I was about fourteen or fifteen years old when I first confronted the visual part of my legacy on a larger scale. One day in high school we were sent to the auditorium to see a movie that had the rather wistful title *Bei Nacht und Nebel* (*Night and Fog*). Great, we thought, we all loved movies, no matter how boring, as long as they got us out of the classroom. The attendance of the principal, however, should have made us suspicious, for his dark suit and somber face was alarming enough. He started to mumble something about Auschwitz, accompanied by the usual nervous coughs. The shoddy black curtain opened and in this morbid, guilt-ridden atmosphere, the darkness of the past crashed down on us—the unforewarned and unprepared.

After seeing the film I was speechless, shocked, and sick to my stomach. We were all sent home without further explanation; I didn't discuss what we'd seen with my classmates, nor did I mention it to my parents. I was so overwhelmed and so numb with revulsion that I was drained of any feelings of outrage toward the perpetrators or pity for the victims. Nothing made sense. Somehow the killers had as little identity as the killed; whenever we had heard something about the Nazis and the Jews, I couldn't find any direct association with my parents or the other older Germans I knew. The film showed the ultimate crime against humanity, and yet for me there was a missing link—

the heart, head, and soul of the machinery, the German people. The grown-ups always gave us the impression that it had just happened. All by itself!

Did those mountains of bodies materialize out of nowhere? And those mountains of hair, eyeglasses, suitcases, shoes, gold teeth, and children's toys? Whose hair was it and who did these things once belong to? Who put them there and why? Where were the hands that locked the doors of the gas chambers, that cut off all that hair, that pulled the triggers, that neatly wrote out the millions of names onto charts and engraved millions of numbers onto forearms?

And where were the heads who thought that up? And where were the people who let it happen? Where are they now—the closed eyes, the shut ears, the sealed lips?

What kind of image of justice and the human condition is created and what moral implications are suggested if adolescents are taught not only that a people can be singled out for mass murder but that such a heinous task can actually be completed without remorse? And together with the smoke of the chimneys in Auschwitz the idea of God blew into the sky and disappeared.

But I didn't only think about what went on in the minds of the hunters; I also thought about the hunted. As a teenager, however, I didn't dare ask what I had wondered about. "But why, what was wrong with them? There *must* have been something wrong with them! They must have done *something* bad! It couldn't be that innocent people can be killed like that!"

Yet I couldn't help wondering why the Jews didn't defend themselves, start a revolution in the concentration camps, get organized, round up the SS and put them in the gas chambers instead. They were the majority, after all. If they

140/      *What Did You Do in the War, Daddy?*

knew that they would die a cruel death—and they must have had at least an inkling after being in the camps for a while—why not die fighting? Why make it so damned easy for their tormentors, why be so obsequiously compliant? I wished so much for the Nazis to be beaten by their victims.

How was I to know that the "final solution" was a nefarious and masterfully planned insanity that eliminated any attempts at rebellion before the victims could even think of it—by the sheer force of the sadism and systematic dehumanization they had had to endure. Being stripped of clothes, hair, dignity, individuality, reduced to a tattooed number worth standing room in a crowded gas chamber, and tortured with roll calls, savage beatings, and humiliation, makes it hard to fight back. The Nazis turned the Jews into creatures who no longer fit within the common norms of civilized society. It was thus easy for them to see the Jews as subhuman, inferior material that should be disposed of, exactly as ordered, without a trace of guilt.

The lingering question "Why the Jews?" never came up in school or anywhere else. Perhaps because we all knew that there was no satisfactory answer to it anyway. I think the standard explanation was something like: Hitler had a crazy obsession with Jews because he was a sick man. His helpers were left unmentioned, faceless. And on those rare occasions when a teacher felt obliged to tell us something about the Jews, only the "presentable" Jewish elite was hastily pointed out to emphasize that Jews were indeed a worthy race, with all those talents like Einstein, Rosa Luxemburg, and Freud. There was no mention of the average, nameless Jews behind the mass anonymity of statistics.

Still, it seems almost impossible to imagine now that I spent most of my teenage years in intense adulation for Kafka and Heine without knowing that they were Jewish.

Even stranger, I didn't know about Anne Frank's existence at all, because neither my teachers nor my parents encouraged me to read her moving diary. It was Hollywood that introduced me to that inspiring Dutch teenager, and all I remember is that it was an incredibly sad story—and that Millie Perkins was such a pretty Anne.

Although I found it difficult for many years to deal with the Nazis and the Holocaust, I nevertheless wanted to see all the documentaries about the Third Reich, some of which contained rare footage of the death camps. I never talked much about what I saw; my sorrow and shame were without words. The images piled up in my mind, but I simply filed them away for the day when I would be able to attach a speck of sense to it all. That day never came.

I once saw a film that had been shot right after the liberation of Buchenwald. Two thousand Germans from nearby villages were forced to walk through the camp and look at the grisly result of what their compatriots had done to other human beings in their name. SS men had once gloated that even if a handful of prisoners did survive, nobody would ever believe their stories, and indeed, in addition to nausea, shock, and disgust, the faces of these German men and women, some pressing handkerchiefs over their mouths, expressed incomprehension. Even when confronted directly by the evidence, the Germans found that the protective mechanism of simply not believing one's eyes worked well, especially for the guilty ones. It couldn't be true! Because if it was, if this had actually happened, then there was no protection from anything. But it did happen and what was once possible might yet become possible again. The truth might be unbearably shattering, but all people, at least once in their lives, should be forced to watch every foot of film that shows the persecution and extermination of the Jews in all its different stages of horror, from *Kristallnacht* to the liberation of the camps.

But all my secret thoughts about Jews and about the Nazi past were buried very deep, and when I came to New York, the last thing I expected was to meet with those whose absence from my life was the manifestation of the reality of genocide. Yet what happens when the descendants of the innocent meet with the descendants of the guilty? Is the innocence of such magnitude that it can swallow the guilt? Or do they both melt and merge to form a coalescence so strong that it can bear the burden of the truth? How many generations does it take—how much atonement and sorrow would allow for forgiveness?

Germans and Jews are intrinsically, emotionally enmeshed with each other, and will be for a long time. Whenever a Jew meets a German, the millions of dead between them take up a lot of space. The German thinks, "I wonder whether he lost a relative in a concentration camp." The Jew thinks, "I wonder whether her father, uncle, or grandfather killed any of us." Both hope for the best, but this spectrum of unsettling, agonizing, unresolved feelings does not make for amicable, trusting, or relaxed friendships.

As it happened, my first American romance was with a Jewish artist, but at the time I didn't know he was Jewish. Jews were still so unreal to me that I couldn't easily visualize them alive or outside of Europe and their black-and-white existence on film. When I learned later that he was Jewish, I was surprised but couldn't help feeling pleased. It was a step in the right direction: personal reconciliation based on love rather than hate, a form of emotional entanglement that doesn't kill.

I would discover that almost all Germans who had spent time in America, especially in New York, had been influenced by their strong and inspiring relationships with Jews, be they troubling and angry encounters or love affairs that sometimes led to marriage. We would even discuss occasionally the ambiguous attraction between Jews and Germans, without dependable scientific results. But we all agreed that meeting face to face with the people who wouldn't be alive at all if our parents' generation had had its way fifty years ago was one of the most significant experiences in our lives, one which the Germans at home could neither match nor fully understand. I have often tried to imagine how my life would have developed without the presence of Jews. Would they have remained to me piles of emaciated bodies? Could I have resurrected them mentally and all by myself just by the power of imagination? Would I have ever felt the need to do so?

The more I talked to Jews my age, the more familiar I became with their backgrounds. Their parents' personal history and their emotional adjustment to the subject of the Holocaust had shaped their perceptions and the degree of hostility and suspicion (or curiosity and openness) that they brought to their encounters with me. Some could never even mention the word "German" at home without eliciting objurgation, outbursts of anger, or obstructive silence, and consequently they had grown weary of the subject or blocked it out completely. Others had developed a strong desire, with or without approval from home, to travel to Germany and meet with Germans, coming back intrigued and favorably impressed.

Some of my friends are first-generation American Jews whose parents had come from Eastern Europe in the twenties and thirties, like the Russian parents of another Jewish friend. When I asked him after our second meeting if he was Jewish, he answered—as I had done many times when asked, "Are you German?"—with a "Why?" instead of a "Yes." I would often meet Jews who weren't crazy about being Jewish, occasionally even trying to cover it up, but I didn't understand their insecurity and lack of pride in their heritage. If it was Germany they were living in, perhaps, but America, tolerant, free-spirited America? Or was it as Kafka once said about Heine: "What is so typically Jewish about him is that he is in conflict with Jewry."

"You don't understand that," a Jewish friend told me. "We are a homeless people. Deep down, we are always on the run, the suitcases are packed in our minds. You never know when the next Holocaust is around the corner. As a little boy, I always dreamt that I was being chased by the SS."

I also began to discover some startling behavioral similarities between my generation and some of my Jewish peers. I owe it to Helen Epstein's stirring book *Children of the Holocaust* that I was able to follow through with some thoughts that I couldn't bring up in the company of Jews. I feared that they might reject the presumptuous notion that a German could claim pain for herself on behalf of the Jews' suffering.

I learned that many children of Holocaust survivors grew up with a throttling silence and an inexplicable fear of a secret box that contained explosive materials and shouldn't be tampered with. These impressions, in turn, reminded me of my own upbringing. The inability of both groups of parents, in my case an entire nation, to speak about the past—one because of pain, the other because of guilt—caused similar symptoms for their offspring. We all accepted our parents' taboo because we were "good" children who wanted to please and protect them. We didn't dare to probe or investigate, but instead we swallowed our curiosity in order to spare our parents their memories.

Through Epstein's book I learned of the special burden of being children of persecuted people who had survived, but I only really knew how it felt to live as a child among the persecutors without ever knowing enough about their victims. On an impulse, then, I decided to attend a private meeting with children of Holocaust survivors, an undertaking that several well-meaning people warned me not to venture into. They feared possible hazard to my soul and equanimity. "Why do you need to do that?" I was asked. "Why don't you?" I replied. Why did I? Because I wanted to be reminded that the truth is still the truth and not an imposition. I didn't feel that it was masochistic exhibitionism on my part but a good opportunity for each side to look at the other and to be exposed to questions and answers that normally don't see the light of day.

There were no fireworks lighting up the synagogue in Queens when my twelve Jewish contemporaries and I sat down together. There was only guarded curiosity on their part and slight tension on mine. I think they couldn't figure out why I came to test waters I might not be able to swim in. But courage is a dependable life ring and I was admired for it after our long discussion.

The setup was certainly not a casual meeting; rather, it had a trial-like quality. To sit opposite people who can say to you with full justification, "How do we know that your father, as an actor, didn't entertain precisely the group of men who would go out the next day and would have killed my parents, if they hadn't been lucky?" was quite a different experience from meeting other American Jews who felt that there was nothing in their personal lives that forced them to grapple with the effects of the Holocaust.

I was also shocked, but not so surprised, by how Germany and the Germans could be perceived by children whose parents had survived the death camps by rare good fortune. That Nazism, like all isms, is an ideology that can be taught, adopted, hammered into people, might be clear to many, but I was confronted with the infuriating assumption that Nazism—or rather, as someone put it, the genetic disposition for malicious killing—is a congenital German disease that is passed on indefinitely to succeeding generations. Which is the same type of theory as the one upon which the Germans based their racial inferiority beliefs and which could also be grounds for the absurd notion that if you can be a congenital killer, you can also be a congenital victim. It is an unsettling feeling to think that someone could take me for a born killer.

A woman close to my age, born in Israel, looked my way, an almost cynical glint in her eyes, and said with impatient anguish, "Look, they killed everybody except my parents— aunts, uncles, grandparents, a large family. No matter how nice you are, I could never set foot in Germany." The fist in my stomach. This was real, not something from the archives, and what a small amount of petty pain for me to endure compared with theirs. I felt silenced, discouraged. I had no reply because there isn't any. I could neither comfort nor blame her, but I thought, "What is she going to tell her children about the Germans and the Germany she might never know? What if her daughter comes home one day and announces, 'I fell in love with a German'?" Yet another person responded, "I can't live with that kind of hatred, it's a crippling feeling."

It is no punishment for me if Jews don't drive German cars or don't grind their coffee beans with a Braun coffee mill, but to collectively reject the German people—and with it, the chance of change—is. I have felt several times like placing myself in front of those who categorically and persistently resist the idea of reconciliation and yelling at them, "What do you want me or us to do? What must we prove and how can we prove it if you don't even want to look at us younger Germans?"

I became aware that their questions about Nazis and Germans, which at times seemed trite and simplistic and which I felt distracted from the real issues, were drawn from an insulated capsule filled with vague suppositions and self-formulated conclusions that were not easy to penetrate. A man who stared at me through his glasses said, "You seem to be an unusual German and your age group is not really a problem, but I wouldn't want to have you around in masses either." He was the same person who asked me, incredulously, "And you didn't grow up hearing people say *Judenschweine* [Jewish pigs] and such?"

On the other hand, I had erroneously assumed that the postwar children of Jewish survivors were particularly knowledgeable about the Nazis and the Holocaust and were obsessed with curiosity and the desire to piece together their parents' past. They were innocent, after all, and had nothing to be ashamed of or afraid of—the way German children might have been. I had thought that only feelings of guilt could produce the repression of unbearable facts, defensiveness, and silence, but I found instead that most younger Jews knew no more about Germans than I had known about Jews before coming to America.

Could it be that both postwar Germans and postwar Jews developed the same diffuse, stereotypical sense of the perpetrators and the victims? Didn't the two observe each other's legacy with the same lack of personal experience and individual encounters? In fact, my Jewish contemporaries and I were introduced to each other's parents' past not through communication but through the written word and through the standard World War II images.

In photos and documentaries we would see the victims as an indistinguishable mass of people herded together, and we would see the persecutors and their adoring acolytes as another mass, with one important difference: not all Germans were Nazis, but all Jews were victims. German teenagers were no less puzzled, awestruck, and deeply distressed than their Jewish counterparts when they witnessed the iniquitous men in riding pants sending "inferior" people into the gas chambers. It was painful for both to realize who our forebears were. The Jews had to live with the images, but I had to live with the people as well.

Once in a while, when talking to skeptical Jews about our mutual conflicts, I get slightly defensive and I feel a little like a chatty sales rep trying to sell a bogus article to people who aren't buying, but it really doesn't matter. That there can't be a "normal" relationship between Germans and Jews may not be so bad after all. A friendship that has to be struggled for, that has to have so many layers of pain, anger, guilt, and suspicion stripped away, has the potential to become a strong, compassionate, and challenging one.

It is our obligation—and ideally a desire—as postwar Germans to move toward the people who were so callously pushed out of our conscience for so long and offer them respect and the spiritual and emotional retribution that our parents' generation denied them by having their government open its wallet instead of offering their hearts. Germans and Jews share a legacy that is like a historical umbilical cord that can't be cut off and that pulls at the most unlikely moments. We younger Germans are innocent as long as we don't forget the past and the guilty ones. One way of redeeming ourselves is to examine the past and to join the fight against allowing crimes of that magnitude ever to happen again. If we can do that, we can turn the burden of our legacy into a blessing. "I have very good German friends," a large number of Jews tell me, and I have become good friends with many Jews. This has been one of my most rewarding achievements in America. There are no two ways about it; we have to step out of the shadow together.

As Marguerite Duras wrote in May 1945 while waiting for her husband to be released from Dachau: "If you give a German and not a collective interpretation to the Nazi horror, you reduce the man in Belsen to regional dimensions. The only possible answer to this crime is to turn it into a crime committed by everyone. To share it. Just like the idea of equality and fraternity. In order to bear it, to tolerate the idea of it, we must share the crime."

# 8

## *Third Reich Reunion*

"Nothing has been proved. There were only some chambers with shower heads on the ceiling that were repeatedly shown to us. Then it was said that gas was let in through these shower heads. Where's the proof? Were you there?"

After recovering from a barely suppressed attack of anger, I looked at my tape recorder, probably expecting it, instead of me, to explode, and then at Peter S., former soldier of the German Wehrmacht and faithful citizen of the Führer and the Third Reich.

No, I wasn't there then, but I am here now, thankful that my birthday was postponed until after the war, preventing me from being a victim *or* a perpetrator.

I grew up among people like Peter S. without realizing what an outstanding, if very suspicious, group was surrounding me, again ruling a country with a questionable credibility that will always be associated with the mechanics of genocide.

I am in a quiet, spotless suburban living room with Peter S. Because I know his son, he could be persuaded to talk to me, even though he felt he had "nothing interesting to tell."

Peter S. was born 1916, in Bremen, into a working-class family. Poverty and hardship were the norm for most Germans in the years after World War I. The bitterness is still there when Peter remembers his mother's struggle to provide for a family of six after separating from his father. Peter apprenticed as an engine fitter and worked as a journeyman until 1935, when he joined the Wehrmacht as a courier pilot. He's a tough-looking little man with thin, greased-back dark hair and beady dark eyes. His outfit is strictly leisure à la pensioner: light blue knit shirt with short sleeves and light gray polyester slacks. This is not a man you dally with or indulge in hypothetical questions about the mysteries of life. This is a no-nonsense proletarian—no frills, no frosting.

When I ask him again about the millions of murdered Jews, he becomes a little impatient but decides to straighten me out. He explains: "After World War I, there were so many rumors about all the horrible things the Germans supposedly did. They were pictured as wolves with knives, cutting off the hands of Belgian and Dutch children. Ridiculous atrocity propaganda. The Germans are always the bad guys. After World War II, the same thing happened. We were the monsters again."

So every photograph we ever saw, every yard of film showing mountains of bodies and people lined up at the ramps is a fake? A case of a bad press? He snaps at me, "This is another question that doesn't belong here. I can explain it in the case of Bergen-Belsen. The English thought it was a German troop camp and bombed it before liberation. Sure, a lot of people got killed; the concentration-camp prisoners had no shelters to go to."

When Peter S. learned about the "final solution" after the war, he knew it couldn't be true; he knew an exaggeration when he heard one. He smacks his lips in a mocking way. "Now, take the so-called six million Jews and quadruple this number. You have the population of one American state."

There are more things that irk Peter. "The Third Reich didn't consist only of war; most people forget that. Before Hitler, there was hunger and unemployment. I was happy when I could join the Wehrmacht. We had a normal, good life. It was the same as being a young man today. One went dancing or to a bar. Politics was the last thing we thought about." He is not impressed with what he feels is an international conspiracy against his perfectly upright countrymen: "The Germans are the scapegoats for everything. When they show old footage on TV, they show only destruction and blame it on the Nazis. But who destroyed Hamburg, Dresden, and Lübeck? Not the bad Nazis but the English and Americans. Just to destroy morale. Nobody's talking about that anymore. We were blamed for not having killed Hitler. Why don't they ask the Russians why they didn't kill Stalin? The people who blame the Germans and Nazis for everything ought to improve themselves. I'm sick of that anti-Nazi propaganda. Look around. War everywhere. Mankind just never learns."

He shakes his head in wonderment about the cruelties and crimes committed in the name of mankind. He never did anything bad. He was just a courier pilot in Hitler's Wehrmacht, flying from front to front. "It was war, and I just did my duty like every other soldier in the world."

Peter S. doesn't feel guilty about anything. How can he, if he doesn't acknowledge the crimes?

My political education is far from being over. I learn from Peter S. that Fascism has nothing to do with National Socialism; that recent worldwide peace demonstrations are organized by the Communists; that, as a matter of fact, members and leaders of all Germany's political parties secretly have a Communist Party membership, even members of the right-wing Christian Democratic Union (CDU); that the Russians are far bigger war criminals than the Germans; and that the Germans never started wars anyway.

Peter is still a soldier at heart. His mind wears a uniform, and the only fitting one belongs to the era of Nazi Germany. Custom-made, and he never outgrew it. He's still on duty, defending Führer and fatherland. It's no miracle to him that Hitler was so successful attacking Europe. No, Adolf had the right approach, and Peter himself wouldn't have done it any differently. He doesn't like cautious characters or worrywarts.

"Before Hitler, Germany had only weaklings who said yes and amen to everything, just like today. Then came Adolf, who started out as a little corporal, something people always used against him, but he told all the other gentlemen a thing or two. He put his foot down and followed through with his plans. The other countries were offended by that, just like they are with Ronald Reagan, who is tough with the Russians. Do you know how many weapons they have stationed in that big country?"

When I throw in that the Führer might not have killed himself if he'd known how many faithful *Volksgenossen* (fellow countrymen) were holding out to the bitter end, his expression changes from triumphant to understanding. "What

154 /     *What Did You Do in the War, Daddy?*

do desperate people do? They commit suicide everywhere—
like this . . . um . . . strange Rainer Werner Fassbinder,
who took sleeping pills with cocaine. Well, there are people
who can't control their lives anymore once they're too famous. After so much shit that happened in the war, it's no
wonder that Hitler killed himself. It was the right thing for
him to do. What kind of a feast would it have been for the
Russians to catch Hitler! What a great propaganda coup to
drag Adolf Hitler on a chain all over Red Square in Mos-
cow!" Just the thought gives him goose bumps.

Peter doesn't extend his sympathy and tolerance to my
generation. He thinks of us as threatening anarchists with
warped ideas and appalling lifestyles, and he is sure that a
certain person's return would take care of this undisciplined
crowd in an appropriate fashion. "Most things are worse
today. Take the *Arbeitsdienst*. It wasn't just an invention of
the Third Reich to draft the youth to work for the benefit
of the country. It was also good for the unemployed young
people to get off the streets and get to work. They were
sent to special projects, and believe me, nobody's dropped
dead by lifting a shovel once in a while. As I said when we
had this enormous flood catastrophe in '62, 'Send the young
men there to help. They have excess energy.' Instead, they
go into the streets, protest against who knows what, create
riots."

Peter leans back in his big TV chair. He feels comfortable. I'm excluded from the aforementioned bunch of weir-
dos because I look neat. He thinks that having too much
freedom leads only to subversiveness, which inevitably
turns into disobedience—a shocking, inconceivable thing
for an orderly German like Peter S. "There has to be an
active commitment for every young person," he says. "It
can be the army. Conscientious objection and all that

bullshit shouldn't be allowed. Some time of one's life has to be sacrificed for homeland and fatherland."

Sacrifice comes easily to Germans of Peter's generation. They don't know anything else. They sacrificed their young lives for a war-hungry egomaniac who discarded them in the end as unworthy of him and for a system that didn't allow for individual dreams and happiness. Peter made the best of it. He feels victimized, but in a different way. Like most older Germans, he feels unjustly accused. "It's always the same. Let's say someone comes into my living room and sees this picture and a swastika [points to a photograph on the wall depicting him in Wehrmacht uniform on his wedding day in 1943] and thinks that I must be a Nazi. Nonsense. What's that got to do with it?"

As the father of two children, he found the same single-mindedness in the school system, where—as little as the teachers mention that uncomfortable past—they paint the Nazi history in the darkest colors. "I don't get involved in that school business anymore. Imagine if I tell my children that everything they learn about the Nazis is rubbish. Right away, the teacher will say, 'Oh, your father was a Nazi too, eh?' The minute someone dares to say that there were very good things too in the Third Reich, they all give it to him. The word 'Nazi' became a slogan for everything bad."

When I suggest that it is not really surprising that the word "Nazi" is rarely used as a compliment, he plays his last card with glittering eyes. "Now let me tell you something. What do the people want from us? I wasn't even a Party member. I was a soldier, and we were not allowed to vote. That's my point. I never gave them my vote, and so I never supported the National Socialist system. Why can't they leave one alone?"

For further protection, Peter S. made a farsighted decision a long time ago. He eliminated any risks. "Under National Socialism, the Communists and Social Democrats were persecuted; after World War II, it was only the Nazis [who were persecuted]. And if this democracy falls apart— and that can happen any day—it will be everybody who is in any party now. I'll never join a party."

A concentration-camp survivor is an unwelcome guest in the conscience-cleared world of postwar Germany. To be a dead victim of the National Socialist regime is much more impressive than to be one of the rare survivors and therefore a living monument with irritating associations.

"The last thing they want to hear about is a true horror story," says Herbert Schemmel, a former political concentration-camp prisoner in Sachsenhausen and Neuengamme. He feels punished by two systems; the postwar government under Konrad Adenauer was the worst, he says. "Not just that it stopped persecuting the Nazi criminals; I never got any compensation or support from it when I needed it after the war. Being 'only' a political prisoner didn't count. It was like an attitude of 'It's your own fault to have been on the left under Hitler.' "

Herbert was born in 1914 and raised in Halle (now in East Germany). He was a well-educated, flamboyant-looking employee in a shipping company, with impeccable manners and without political ambitions—just membership in a leftist union. His background was comfortably middle-class with a Social Democratic tradition. The Nazis were thoroughly despised and not taken too seriously by his family.

After Herbert refused to participate in the National Socialist "Day of National Labor" on May 1, 1933—an obli-

gation for all working people—the Gestapo invited him for
a brief visit, but nothing extreme happened. Still, he decided to disappear to Leipzig, where he worked without
interference in a well-paid job until September 1, 1939, the
day the war broke out. A blacklist of three hundred names,
his among them, brought the brutal Gestapo back into the
picture and marked the beginning of an uninterrupted or-
deal that would last until the end of World War II.

"I was arrested on charges of 'defeatist remarks' and 'un-
dermining actions against the National Socialist state.' God,
was I beaten up by those pigs. I learned that I had insulted
the swastika flag. I used to park my BMW car in an underground garage. Just above the entrance was the meeting room of the Hitler Youth, with a flag hanging down
very low, so it almost got trapped once in my car door.
I had said to a boy I knew there, 'Klaus, you should
hang the flag a bit higher. And besides, it needs to be
washed too.' "

It is still a source of bitterness that he had actually been
denounced by several people. "The Gestapo had a list with
every single sentence I'd ever said. Colleagues, acquain-
tances, and my own secretary stabbed me in the back. It
was devastating."

A very nervous, restless man, Herbert grows even more
agitated. His eyes dart around aimlessly, his hands are
either in his pockets playing with his keys or wiping imaginary crumbs from the empty desk. He gets up every few
minutes and paces.

After he was arrested, he tells me, "I was tried at the
newly installed *Sondergericht* [special court for political
crimes] and acquitted because of insubstantial evidence.
Outside the court, the Gestapo was already waiting for me
with a red 'protective custody' order, signed by Reinhard

Heydrich [Gestapo deputy chief]. I had heard terrible things about Dachau and other concentration camps, but the reality I was to experience was incomprehensible."

His still-handsome features grow tense as he recalls his transition, in a matter of hours, from a healthy, self-assured, elegantly dressed young businessman into a dehumanized, beaten shadow of an identity with shorn hair and striped clothes. These few hours, during which reality switched from tolerable normality to unimaginable horror, are engraved on his brain like the numbers on the prisoners' forearms.

"My destination was Sachsenhausen. We were seventy-five men on the bus—anything from criminals, homosexuals, and politicals to a few Jews. After we arrived, the very young SS guards were beating us brutally, at random. Then they started asking, 'Why are you here?' My neighbor, accused of having sexual relations with a minor, could only say, 'I like little girls. . . .' He was beaten to death right next to me."

The beautiful English-tweed coat with white flecks that Herbert was wearing became a symbol of the ferociously fast deprivation of his freedom between sunrise and dusk. "I had to lie down on the dirty ground, roll around, jump up and do knee bends, hands behind the head, called *Sachsen-Gruss* [Saxon salute]." He gets up and demonstrates. "My coat was black after that. I mean black." Then, together with the coat and a gold wristwatch, he handed over his civilization and dignity for the next six years. He laughs a hysterical laugh, but it still breaks his heart.

Compared to what was to follow, daily life in the "political block" seemed almost passable. But once the "camp *Führer*" received Herbert's file from the Gestapo, he was suddenly put into "punitive custody"—apart from the main camp—for three months. Which meant that he was as good as dead.

"We were seventy-two Germans from all categories. Three SS men were guarding us around the clock, beating us most of the time. The *Kapo* [highest-ranking prisoner] was a mass murderer. We didn't work but had a daily rate of seventeen deaths—starved or tortured to death by one of the many varieties of heinous inventions." One favored pastime for the SS was locking prisoners into a broom closet sealed with wet blankets. There was no way that anyone would come out alive.

When Herbert wasn't engaged in senseless physical activities called "sport"—standing for endless hours, rolling around on the ground and running back and forth—he had to carry the deceased to the crematories. "Of course, bureaucracy was the most important thing. All that counted was that the dead were registered. The number was written with a pen on their naked bellies. Legibly."

In 1940, a high-ranking political prisoner arranged for him to go on a transport to construct a new concentration camp in Neuengamme, near Hamburg. "You see here a man who built his own concentration camp," he says, laughing. "We worked night and day. Naturally, we had to build the foundations of every good concentration camp first: the roll-call square and the electric fence." His knowledge of typing and mathematics gained him a position as chief clerk, the most sought-after job in the camp because it excused one from the feared outside labor.

He wasn't beaten anymore and dreamed about the day of liberation. "I had a lot of repressed hatred and wrath, but I wanted to live through the next day. That was our philosophy. Resistance was useless. The SS were killers, brutal slaughterers."

It was Gestapo chief Heinrich Himmler's practical perversion to preserve as many worthy laborers as possible by creating active entertainment: from 1942 on, skinny striped silhouettes were allowed to play soccer on Sunday afternoons, were able to form a camp band, and were offered sexual pleasures. In 1944, twelve women prisoners moved into what became the camp brothel. One had to be waitlisted three weeks in advance and earn the opportunity through tireless work and impeccable behavior. Many wanted to visit, but not for sex.

"Sex was the last thing we would dream about. Our physical condition was so bad that it wouldn't have been possible anyway. The brothel had the best-heated, cleanest rooms; it was just nice to sit there awhile."

Herbert escaped from Neuengamme in May 1945, before it was liberated. Fifty-five thousand people were killed there in five years. It is astounding that, as a native of nearby Hamburg, I never heard of Neuengamme, either in school or anywhere else, until ten years ago. For thirty-five years, until 1981, the government of Hamburg refused to build a memorial on the grounds of the destroyed concentration camp. But psychological satisfaction and compensation, justice and democracy didn't materialize for Herbert in postwar Germany.

"The government under Adenauer treated former political prisoners like shit. It's unbelievable how much corruption and injustice there was under him. From 1950 on, most war criminals were reprieved by the Americans and the Russians, and the trials practically stopped. The CDU had, and still has, plenty of former SS men as members. Adenauer's Secretary of State, Hans Globke, helped formulate the Nuremberg Laws, and another minister was the head of an extermination group in the East. Both resigned eventually in the sixties—without any hard feelings. The pensions they received were not insubstantial."

Herbert still works part-time for an import-export firm but doesn't have his own office. We sit in a big, cluttered storage room, filled with Japanese junk. He paces through the room as he sarcastically describes German justice: "Thank God that Richard Bugdalle, chief of punitive custody of Sachsenhausen, has no worries. He was sentenced to life in prison—I was the prime witness at his trial—but he was released after a few years. He lives now in a nifty state home for old people. The government pays half the rent."

Herbert never received a pfennig in restitution money before he was sixty-five years old. Hypocrisy and double standards were the norm when it came to the great cash-in after the war. "The classification for the political prisoners [for restitution payments] was based on their status three years prior to imprisonment. What that meant for the people who were sent to camp in 1933 is obvious: they were, of course, unemployed in 1930. I was lucky that I had a good job [before being imprisoned] and that I'm twenty percent disabled because of an injured hand."

Herbert also remembers another German postwar classic, the "I was never for the Nazis" syndrome. As a member of the Committee for Political Prisoners after 1945, he helped sort out the growing number of so-called victims. "Suddenly, they were *all* political prisoners—the SS too," he remarks dryly.

Is Herbert at peace with himself and the past? He has a happy marriage, grown-up children, and a financially comfortable life. Herbert looks me in the eye for the first time in three hours, then frowns and looks away. "We were hoping the Nazis would be eliminated after the war. The opposite was the case. What do I know who my neighbor is?"

As an honored member of the Neuengamme Foundation, he shows school classes and other groups around his old concentration camp. The younger people show great interest, he says. "But in a way, it is all unimaginable for them. When I show them photos with the corpses and the human skeletons, I tell them, 'This is not a fiction, this is reality.' "

"The past is gone," says Günther F., a journalist and former Party member and Waffen SS soldier. "There must be an end to it. I can't change what happened, and I'm not responsible for it."

But Günther F. is anything but at ease with the past. He doesn't have the cheeky impudence of Peter S. and would rather banish forever that whole chapter from his mind. But since he agreed to talk to me, he decided to prepare for the event. A box with photographs he took during the Third Reich, newspaper clippings, and even his denazification certificate awaited me, and he was eager to explain the memorabilia.

The German living room is like an institution. Pleasure and duty are combined in an unoriginal way: TV and easy chair, a couch with pillows under a serious oil painting. Hanging on the wall are color photographs of wife, children, and grandchildren, and on the bookshelves is anything from Heinrich Böll to Albert Speer. A special niche is reserved for the fatally unlucky hour of German resistance—books about the attempted assassination of Hitler and about the heroes who were killed for trying.

Günther F. is a tall, slim, and sober-looking man. His thin black hair is combed back neatly, and his gold-framed glasses cover uncertain-looking eyes. He has a friendly, though insecure, smile; he isn't quite sure whether it was the right idea to talk about the things "that are so far back and forgotten" with someone who wasn't even there. But we are almost colleagues.

Born in Pomerania in 1913, he worked as an editor-journalist in Frankfurt before he was assigned to create a front newspaper for the German Wehrmacht in occupied Estonia in 1941. He shows me a faded yellow issue of his paper, which he put together almost entirely by himself for four years.

It was a great time for him: adventurous, challenging, and dangerous. He holds up the front page, full of the usual fabrications from the Reich: victory after victory . . . a triumphant-looking Führer . . . *wunderbar, Sieg Heil* . . . we just attacked the Soviet Union. Column after column filled with penetrating propaganda from the insidious mind of Goebbels, Hitler's Minister of Culture. And sickest of all are the countless obituaries, or rather thank-you notes from grateful parents "who are honored that their son was allowed to give his life to the Führer."

Günther F. isn't troubled by the fact that he never fulfilled the ideal of journalism: truth telling. "I liked the creativity and responsibility of it, and I was glad not to be in the infantry," he says. He was told via Berlin what the daily slogans were to be. Not only did he carry out his orders to his superiors' satisfaction and with great eagerness and enthusiasm, but they coincided perfectly with his own convictions.

Günther F. joined the Party and the Waffen SS in 1932. He and his parents believed in and supported the new National Socialist movement. "Hitler was fascinating, and Germany's economic, political, and cultural rise was fantastic. The 1936 Olympic Games were spectacular, and the whole world thought so too. Nobody interfered when Hitler attacked Europe."

Like most Germans, Günther feels ambivalent about the Führer: Adolf Hitler was quite a guy, had the right ideas about youth, art, economy, church, education, and philosophy. "Hitler was likable because he remained simple. . . . I attribute the best of intentions to him," Günther says.

"As a soldier, you just don't know a thing. Do you know what our government has in store for us right now? It's the same situation now as it was before World War II. It can be repeated, in a different way, of course. One crazy guy will push the button. And then it will be your generation, if someone is still alive, that will be asked, 'Didn't you see it coming? Couldn't you stop it?' "

Oh, these contradictions. In between his precarious, incoherent, often offensive answers, he comes up with valid questions.

"I was a POW of the Americans, and we were held at a former concentration camp, Flossenburg—that's how I know that all the gassing of the Jews is true. We saw the gas chambers—and I remember the sixth of August 1945. A sergeant from Oklahoma came in and said, 'We just dropped the atomic bomb.' Who is responsible for those bombs in Hiroshima and Nagasaki?"

Günther F. is now retired but still writes articles for local newspapers in Frankfurt, where he lives. He enjoys the remaining fragments of pure German *Kultur* whenever he can. Which isn't as often as it used to be, since TV, radio, magazines, and practically everything else is infiltrated with foreign elements. He looks back longingly to the time when culture was purged of non-Germanic elements, when books were burned, "decadent art" was banned, and when Goebbels set the standards for all the artless cultural mediocrities to come. It is wishful thinking to believe that the denunciation and removal of all non-Germanic elements in the entire cultural sphere created any uproar.

"I wasn't aware that so many things were forbidden," Günther says. "I didn't miss them. I liked the fact that they banned all those American songs we're swamped with again today. Do we have to listen to 'White Christmas' on Christmas Day in Germany? I didn't like jazz, I didn't like *The Threepenny Opera*, and I was glad that these decadent plays were no longer around. I still have no understanding or liking for the degenerate paintings. They really don't fit in. I have no use for a Picasso, where a woman's breast is on her kneecap and that kind of thing."

He laughs as he remembers an anecdote: "My father owned a framing workshop. It was mostly the Jews who brought in these kinds of pictures. My father would say, 'If you accept a framing job, don't forget to ask where the hook goes.' We couldn't figure out which side was up or down." He is still laughing when he adds, "I personally could sketch real well and knew about art."

The Germans might not have come to grips with their past or grasped its complexity and its eternal effects, but they seem to be at peace with one thing: that they are Germans, unchanged and unashamed. They remain faithful to their self-proclaimed national character and rarely recognize the psychological connection of who they are with what happened and why.

"Yes, we are obedient and accept authority," Günther says. "But that is everywhere in the world." He has his own theory about the hostility he has experienced while visiting foreign countries, especially the formerly occupied ones. "We are disliked because we are efficient, capable, thorough people. Well, we are also arrogant. That is typically German. They all begrudge us our success—that we made it after the war. We might be a nuisance, but the world needs us—we're important." But Günther doesn't exude much self-importance. He sounds mostly helpless and hopeless. Still, his robust Teutonic disposition triumphs over the frail shadows of doubt. Is Günther a typical German? Now, that comes close to an insult, but his good humor returns. "No, no. I'm not a typical German. I'm tolerant."

The other side of tolerance is blindness and silence. Who was to blame and who are the guilty ones?

"The people who did it were responsible, the people who were punished for it," he says. "I don't feel guilty at all. Collective guilt doesn't exist." With a German, it is not easy to pin down the nebulous identity of the mysterious phantoms "who were really guilty." Günther feels cornered: "The elite SS troops in the camps were exceptional sadists. It erupted in them."

The Weimar Republic is blamed for Hitler's rise to power. There was no peace movement of great impact before and between the wars. Wars were part of life. The impact of parents, upbringing, and milieu during World War I and the Weimar years from 1919 to 1933 are reduced to vague memories of contentment.

"My father didn't recount any critical or horrible stories when I was a kid," Günther says. "There were no antiwar talks. He did his duty, just like I did. He told us funny, entertaining stories."

Of course, there must have been sad stories too. "But why should he tell those? We didn't talk about war then, and we don't talk about war now—I, my family and friends."

His cheerfulness is long gone. Looking back holds no comfort for him. "I worry about the present and the future. There are many things I don't like, mainly our government, but I can't change that. I also don't understand why so many innocent people have to die today. And how about recent terrorism in Germany? . . . Look at the world now. The past is gone, but the politicians all over the world didn't learn a thing."

Günther F. disclaims any responsibility for truthfully informing his two children, born in 1947 and 1949. "Talking about the past leads only to glorification and heroism. I know the war adventures of my working colleagues inside out. What heroes they were!" This strange logic of why a father has no other choice than to glorify war is not understandable right away, but Günther F. feels attacked and gets very curt. "It was beyond discussion. Besides," he says of his children, "they didn't ask."

His children gave up asking. No wonder. "Sure, they have the right to know about the past, but do I have the duty to tell them about all the atrocities?" he wonders. "Our right was to forget about the past and start anew."

This position struck me as intolerable; nothing justifies this irresponsible failure of parents who bore us into a vacuum expecting us to fill the space. My generation does share one sense of loss with Günther F.: "I have no feelings of strong national identity anymore," he says, "nothing I want to get involved in. We're suffocating in weapons, and I'm afraid that they're going to use them one day."

Günther reassures me that his past doesn't hold any demons for him anymore—except for the recurring horrible dreams he still has about "crashing bombs, sirens, and fire." But it takes a stronger jolt to frighten a German war survivor than just a nightmare. "Oh, they're nothing serious," he says. "I always escape unharmed."

When I first encountered Werner Lansburgh, a Jewish author born in Berlin in 1912, I was in the audience and he was reading from his recent book, *Dear Doosie*, a collection of satirical, sharp-witted reflections on Jewish-German-Swedish life, written in German mixed with English. Luckily, he had escaped the gas chambers and the cruelties of life under the Third Reich. He emigrated in 1933, when he was a twenty-one-year-old student, first to Spain, where he supported the Loyalists, and then to Sweden, where he stayed away for forty-five years from the country he still loves—though with a degree of ambivalence. His attempts to return to Germany failed many times because of subconscious fear and his failure to find a job. Since 1979, he has lived in Hamburg and now feels happier than ever, because the instant success of his book marked his final exit from Sweden, where he had longed for Germany.

Germany? How could one get homesick for a country where the "final solution" was invented, where one's own potential murderers still reside? How could he trust his contemporaries? Werner's answer is as surprising as it is touching:

"I am a German. And if there is such a thing as collective guilt, I'll have to accept my part of it. I do identify myself with this country. Who knows whether I might've become a Nazi if I'd been born an Aryan?"

We sit in Werner's spacious, old-fashioned apartment. Its relaxed atmosphere is a pleasant departure from the usual mass-fabricated suburban homes of the *Wirtschaftswunder* years.

This fragile-looking man with thick white hair knows about conflicts. "The Germans have two souls in their breast, as Goethe's *Faust* suggests. Thomas Mann even wrote an essay called 'Brother Hitler.' I was not so different from everybody else. I left a bitter and therefore cruel and uncivilized country. And I was part of this 'uncivilization.' "

Werner's background is typical of well-educated, assimilated Berlin Jews. He lovingly describes his father, a famous professor of economics, as a "right-wing liberal, very progressive and critical." Werner, a talented whiz kid, used to hang out in left-wing intellectual and artists' circles in Berlin. He and his Jewish friends were "so assimilated, we wanted to be Germans first and would rather not have been Jews at all."

Werner's father saw the writing on the wall early and urged his son to leave in 1933. He himself committed suicide in 1937, one year after being forced to give up his position as a professor. In 1938, Werner managed to get his mother out of Germany and into Sweden, where they were joined by his sister, who had managed to stay in the underground in Berlin until 1944.

It is hard for a lot of people, including myself, to understand why the Jews weren't alarmed before the start of such violent actions as the *Kristallnacht* in November 1938. The degrading restrictions had already begun in 1933 with the exclusion of Jews from public office, the civil service, teaching, the theater, and journalism, followed by the even more repressive Nuremberg Laws in 1935. Yet it isn't surprising for Werner.

"The Jews really believed they could live in Germany. The Nazis didn't want to attack them too brutally at once, because regular citizens would have been shocked. Gradually, the Nazis tightened the reins. The chicanery was pretty obvious, but the Jews just didn't want to believe that any of the threats and prophesies would come true. Most thought the specter would disappear."

Werner blames the conditions under the Weimar Republic for the instant success of the anti-Semitic National Socialist propaganda and the public's susceptibility, because "Germans were a bitter people who needed a scapegoat." The Jews were the perfect material because, as Werner puts it, with a little grin, "it is typical of the Jews that they can do anything. They are multi-talented, versatile, and skillful. Anything from Bernstein to Einstein is there. They also had the money and owned banks. There were also a lot of Jews from Eastern Europe who bought up whole streets for a few zloty and who were conspicuous—unlike the millionaires and armament big shots in their castles. These things helped Goebbels a lot and lent substance to anti-Semitism."

Even more dangerous than the Jewish businessmen were the intellectuals on the left. "They were too challenging for the German bourgeoisie," he says. "The German is a reactionary, he's a real bourgeois. One has to be careful not to provoke him. And that provocation came from the radical left, which often happened to be Jewish."

That's when the talents of Hitler came into the picture—a man, Werner says, "whose real genius was that he was the incarnation of a petty bourgeois with some exaggeration." To Werner the creation of National Socialism was ingenious. "For the simple worker, it offered primitive anti-capitalism, but in such a way that big shots like Thyssen and Krupp could participate too. It was anti-intellectual, so even the modest mind felt at home. Back-to-nature, restoring the 'blood and soil' tradition—that was something for the farmers, who loved Hitler. The Jews represented the city and commerce."

Hitler's allure is not such a phenomenon to Werner. He feels the Führer didn't simply seduce a whole nation with extraordinary, cunning tricks; all he had to be was his natural self. "Like many others, I didn't take him seriously. He was around for some time. I practically grew up with Hitler. He fit perfectly into the general mold of German brutality. He was a regular representative of his people. Just one of them," Werner says, shrugging his shoulders.

Could there have been any Jews who liked Hitler? "Some might have found Hitler impressive as a person," he says. "There were Jewish Nazi sympathizers who said, 'It's only fair, what happened to us.' We called them the *raus mit uns Juden* [out with us Jews].

"When we heard about the concentration camps where thousands of Jews were being gassed every day—it was around '43—we didn't want to believe it. I worked with the British embassy, and they received photos and eyewitness reports from survivors. Neither the Americans, the Germans, nor the Jews wanted to believe it."

After the war, when there was no doubt left, Werner had a haunting recollection. "It confirmed what I had already foreseen as a little boy. In the Weimar Republic, physical education had been a main subject in school. The tradition of drill was already there—it didn't come with the Hitler Youth—and I hated it. And I had wild dreams about people who were slaughtered. It was very mystical. With the extermination of the Jews, my pernicious dreams came true."

After the war, when the Germans woke up from *their* nightmare and started dreaming again, did it mean that they had changed?

"I returned to Germany because I didn't find anything better," he says. "I'm a writer, and this is my language." He wants to believe in changes because he believes in himself and feels it is his role to bring a "refined British touch" to the uncivilized Germans. He also believes in my generation because it "changed the tenor, the militaristic atmosphere inside and outside the family that had been the tradition in the Weimar Republic."

"Has Germany really changed?" he wonders. "Sometimes I ask myself whether it's just a great paint job—when you scratch long enough, the old color shines through."

My interview with Werner triggered a lot of mixed emotions. He was the first German Jew I ever met. Jews were rare in Germany—they had either left or been gassed. A German Jew seemed like an ideological and psychological contradiction to me. Like being the victim and perpetrator in one.

I realized that Werner and I were facing the same conflict. We both mistrust Germans, yet we both are Germans. My mistrust was initiated by historical facts and confirmed by personal experience, his by being born in 1912. He had suffered a lot, but he expressed much less wrath than I did. Do pain and injustice make people forgiving? Not trusting the Germans meant not trusting myself unless I believed in change and in the power to shape one's destiny. Ironically, Werner was one of only two people I talked with who had considered the questions of personal and collective guilt. He had accepted the latter.

After traveling in Germany for half a year and talking to many elderly German fathers, my feelings remained ambiguous on many levels. They were the trying group I had been prepared for—stubborn, resilient, priggish relics with much endurance and little compassion. They often amazed me with the kind of inimitable, unintentional deadpan humor, Hitleresque diction, and rhetorical chutzpah that only these hard-boiled Wehrmacht veterans could produce. Still, their iron will and determination to survive, to start again and face life undeterred—despite their past—had my respect.

Who would envy them? Born before, during, or after World War I, they are a prewar and a postwar generation in one, being the children of the tumultuous Weimar Republic and growing slowly into the creators and citizens of the Third Reich. The luxury of choice was never theirs. The "best years of their lives" were a waste and a sacrifice. While other young men in their twenties and thirties were exploring their minds, seeking out adventures, reaching for the stars, those young Germans were lined up in army uniforms, marching toward war and destruction. Survive or die. Simple as that.

And yet, they defend a time that, in the end, brought them only pain and loss. They refuse to feel betrayed, for it would make them look like fools and tools. But they also refuse responsibility, because it would make them feel guilty.

To have nothing left to show from a twelve-year period but war wounds, a few unpresentable decorations, and a box of dusty photographs depicting smiles under the swastika that will never make it to the walls of their children's and grandchildren's living rooms, is a depressing reward. No, those were not the victorious years. A nation marched over its legendary human and cultural achievements and left nothing greater to celebrate than the Volkswagen and the *Autobahn*.

When I drove back to the airport on one of these famed roads, I left behind an unfinished puzzle. The detective in me knew that this case couldn't be resolved now. And probably never will.

# 9

## *No Sorrow and No Pity*

I had often wondered why older Germans didn't suffocate from their emotional restraint. Where had they put their guilt and shame? Their denial of segments of their past has left traces on their and our characters; we inherited their ambivalences.

Because of the nearly total repression of the subject, we younger Germans were never able to feel outraged and shocked by our parents' and country's complicity in the deeds of the Third Reich. When we saw concentration-camp footage on TV, we couldn't scream, we couldn't explode with anger and rage, we couldn't express anything that would even begin to echo the magnitude of the horrible crimes. If you're not told about loss, if no one around you feels sadness, shame, or pity, you become mute as well.

But so many of us gagged on this undigested emotional ballast that an explosion grew inevitable. As a result, a large part of the generation born between 1940 and 1950 took its rage to the streets in the student revolt of 1967–68 and the

RAF (Red Army Faction) terrorism that followed. We wanted to hear ourselves, to feel that we had voices, and through this collective loud scream of my peers erupted the unacknowledged, massively repressed reality of the Third Reich with double strength and in a sometimes exaggerated form. But our parents should have been the ones to scream about what had happened in their name. Was it our destiny to do it for them? Were we the deputies for their repressed fury? Many people of both generations went to the streets to take a stand—for opposite reasons and with different consequences. They should have cheered their children when they demanded an end to the war in Vietnam, risking a police club on our heads and occasionally arrest. They should have joined us. Why didn't both generations unite in a powerful crusade against war, oppression, injustice, and inhumanity?

Didn't we do what they proclaim they would have done if Hitler's deadly dictatorship hadn't prevented even modest expressions of protest? They finally had a chance to prove their courage and political maturity, and what did they do? They took a seat in the audience, and while we fought the Establishment, they called the cops. They must have felt envy when they observed that we made opposition possible.

To some extent, though, I am grateful to the Nazi generation for driving me to discover rebellion and a taste for anarchy—and I loved it. Protest became an important form of expression for me, and by 1968 I had started screaming, yelling, hooting, and cursing. After *that* past, to roam the streets and to demonstrate an opinion was exhilarating, healing, and, for the moment, liberating. I craved disobedience and upheaval, something emotionally rewarding that promised radical social and political improvement. After the forever lingering stench of Prussian military drill, the bureaucratic mentality, and a decade of insane dictatorship, the iconoclastic outburst by the mutinous German youth of the late sixties was a hurricane of fresh air that was as dizzying as its exuberance was contagious.

Feeling mentally disconnected from my uninspiring environment—which had been built and controlled by the Nazi burghers—made it impossible for me to desire anything less than a "New Order." I was swept away by lofty ideas and not at all intimidated by false respect and conventional consideration for parents, the state, or other authorities. I have to admit, however, that it wasn't only worthy causes that drove me to the streets and made me a passionate demonstrator. I approached the whole thing instinctively and with a zeal for the action itself that sometimes transcended the content. When in doubt, I was against it, particularly when "it" was the Establishment and the injustices of the world. All I knew about Vietnam was that wars always meant genocide and that the American invasion of another country was an evil act. This was motivation enough to march enthusiastically behind anti-Vietnam banners and to scream extemporaneous rhymes at the stoic-looking policemen. To help build a new political consciousness I was prepared to get arrested (luckily, I never was) and to take abuse from old people everywhere, who responded to our unruly uprisings with predictable pearls of wisdom, like "And we taxpayers have to support you anarchistic hippies."

My unceremonious relationship to politics led me to favor actions that were provocative yet simple—actions that could not be misunderstood. In 1968, for example, Germany's Chancellor was Kurt Georg Kiesinger—the incarnation of an ultraconservative, smooth, but thoroughly detestable man. And one day, during a Christian Democratic Union rally in Berlin, a very unassuming-looking young German woman named Beate Klarsfeld, fast as lightning and out of nowhere, darted onto the speaker's tribune and gave Kiesinger a hearty slap on his face while calling him "Nazi."

I saw this on the evening news and screamed with delight, "Right on, Beate!" I didn't even know about Kiesinger's Nazi past (he was a Nazi Party member), but I was certain that he deserved to be slapped in public. I was also immediately aware of the significance of the event, for it meant more than simply disobedience against the state authority. Here, a daughter was symbolically slapping a Nazi father in front of all of Germany. That a woman had chosen such a simple technique and such a pompous and misogynistic scenario as a party rally endeared her even more to me. Whenever I look back at the sixties, Beate Klarsfeld's fearless slap remains peerless.

As stunning as the sixties phenomenon was in its universality, the European student rebellions of '68 nonetheless arose from radically different historical roots from those in America. Our countries had been in ruins; our parents were victims, perpetrators, and survivors. More than anything else, though, Germany's rebellious sixties were a reaction to our fathers.

Although physically present, our fathers were not available to us as role models, heroes, and emotional supporters; we were thus a fatherless generation as well as a "homeless" generation—discontented, isolated, and quite lonely. But on the streets we were no longer alone—I felt as if I were part of a large surrogate family and I finally felt solidarity with other people who stood for unification, a defiant spirit, and challenging ideas. When I looked at my fellow twenty- to twenty-five-year-olds, I saw fierce, angry, and hurt faces. The lack of roots and pride had made us feel incomplete—

maybe on the streets, in communes, and in universities we could at last embrace each other and become whole again.

We had no other choice, we *had* to be rebellious, for this was our only chance to prove that we were different. We had so much to rebel against: our parents' undigested past, the new "democracy" that allowed old Nazis to hold high positions, and a government that pushed legislation through the Bundestag that barred suspicious, "subversive" people like us from official employment. Generally, the relations between young and old in Germany are still defined by an insurmountable distrust. They don't trust us, we don't trust them. They've been punished for trusting a man and a system, we've been punished by having them as politicians and fathers.

I grew up with the children of Nazis, and although I later lived with them in communes and protested with them on the streets, I never felt any mistrust toward them, because we all had crawled out of that big Nazi pot and the damage had affected all of us. Discussions were severe and dogmatic, led by long-haired young men with wild eyes and tense faces (women served the tea) who sputtered out certain theories about the "enemy property." They also held a strange, very presumptuous belief that they shared the struggle of people under dictatorships and other political terror in South America and the rest of the Third World. Considering the German tradition of political self-ignorance, this search for faraway causes wasn't so surprising. Not once did anybody ask about someone else's father or volunteer information about his or her own. We took the world apart, condemned evil governments, pointed fingers at oppression and inhumanity—but we couldn't look into the hearts and minds of those who had raised us; we simply imitated our parents, who didn't discuss their past with each other either. In all the activity of freeing our minds, dropping out and tuning in, we had forgotten where we came from.

Where the sixties failed was in not coming to grips with our parents' past, and our own, because the New Left failed to see the specificity of the Third Reich and the Holocaust. In the end the goal of the rebellion lacked sharp focus because sheer rage was disguised as politics. It simply didn't progress beyond a primitive form where reflection had no part, and it seemed impossible at that time to fill the highly emotional framework with sensible, homogenous content and lucid visions. Because of the fact that not much changed fast and the genuine search for the self didn't happen, the disillusionment was great and came rapidly—as if old structures can be smashed in one delirious, revolutionary year—and many Germans turned to aggression, fanaticism, and bitterness.

I think that to a large extent the form and the content of the sixties protest were more a neurotic expression than the wish to change the world. If one compares it with psychoanalysis, then this is a case where the patient broke off the treatment prematurely. We were only in our early twenties, the ones who had grown up shielded from the recent past and didn't know that it isn't enough to want to rebel because you're young; true rebellion, the spiritual kind that brings along healthy changes, is an ongoing process that is never completed. For many of us, it had only begun.

I often had the disturbing feeling that the Germans hadn't been punished enough for those terror years. I didn't know exactly how they ought to be punished, but I felt it unset-

tling, almost frightening that Germany had never pro-
gressed beyond recognizing the wrath of the survivors
against their oppressors.

Occasionally there are still trials, usually unsensational,
sluggish ones. But the accused never remember whether
they killed "only" ten or thirty or five thousand people. "It's
been such a long time," they say, and scratch their heads.
It doesn't seem to bother most old Germans that Nazi war
criminals are usually acquitted and return to their carefree
lives. Was this a sign of accepting their own guilt—letting
the killers go unpunished, allowing them to participate in
a so-called democracy?

It is not unusual for people to feel the urge to escape
from the burden of tormenting memories. The Germans
falsified, blocked, repressed, and fabricated the reality of
Nazi Germany and the role they played in it. It's hard for
them to bear that a period of time when self-glorification
and dreams of omnipotence almost became reality has also
been inextricably connected with the greatest crimes. Their
egos wouldn't permit them to integrate the unvarnished
truth into their present life. Instead, they worked out a
psychological trick, a form of protective schizophrenia, in
order to escape their crimes and culpability. Without denying the past completely, they separated themselves from
the deeds—it wasn't really they who did anything wrong,
it was that "other" part inside of them that automatically
answers to authority, independent of individual judgment.
"That human beings can do such things," I often heard
them complain, shaking their heads in disbelief over these
"other" monsters in human disguise. They still cannot admit that they themselves created the emotional climate and
the political base that allowed these crimes to be committed.

Unfortunately, in the Germans Hitler had a people who were able to function with the conscience switched off and the programmed obedience switched on.

A scary but perfect example of the twisted way in which most Germans separated and absolved themselves from physical and moral complicity is Rudolf Höss, commandant of Auschwitz. Like all Nazi war criminals, he felt that he was a victim of his virtue. This virtue was obedience. Höss seems the embodiment of the generic Nazi when he points out, "Personally, I had never anything against Jews. I don't know the feeling of hatred." He even tries to transform heinous murder into personal tragedy by expressing feelings of sorrow for the poor, helpless children who had to be sacrificed to the gas chambers. But he doesn't have feelings of guilt. "I personally never approved of the cruelties in the concentration camps. I never ever killed a prisoner or tortured one."

I don't think that the majority of the Germans had extraordinarily strong personal feelings of hatred against Jews. Actually, on one level it would have been less horrible if they had been motivated by real conviction. Then at least their participation in the persecution and killing of the Jews would have been a crime of passion. But the cool fanaticism was focused on the perfect performance, not the content. What killed the Jews was less the Germans' hatred than their love for obedience.

After the Germans had killed their Jews—even that "single decent" Jew whom, according to an indignant Himmler, every German seemed to have known—they were incensed about *the way* it had happened—not so much that it had happened at all. Many Germans felt appalled by mass extermination, not because it was the organized murder of totally *innocent* people, but because it was connected to so much cruelty, abuse, and violence. Nobody wanted that. Like Höss, they felt that no good, upright German should lower himself by torturing Jews, but he should perform his duty correctly and properly—just impersonal, orderly shootings or straight and clean gas-chamber work without sadistic interludes. And yet for others it would have been sufficient and more humane to have gotten rid of the Jews in the way a former Stalingrad doctor once suggested to me: "They should have been given money and forced to leave the country within a few weeks. That would have been fair and much wiser."

With this cruel attitude it is no wonder that the Germans have been incapable of mourning, since it requires sadness and a sense of loss. A person can only mourn something that was valuable to him and with which he had an emotional relationship. Consequently, the Germans had to maintain their negative image of the Jews because the recognition that they were equals, worthy enough to be missed, and that six million people had to die innocently is so unbelievably horrifying and iniquitous that their conscience still rebels against it. But most of all, mourning would require an active awareness of the death of the Jews and that would reinforce guilt.

But beyond the millions of people they killed, the Germans find any sort of mourning impossible. Even the losses of fellow soldiers and family members have not found expression in a people whose own sense of self-worth is so deflated. There is no distinction between the cold, pitiless way they treat others and the way they treat themselves. Although uncommonly arrogant on the surface, the older Germans are deep down full of insecurity and self-contempt—the other side of grandiosity and arrogance.

I firmly believe that the alarming precision and naturalness with which the Germans in the camps and in the many murderous *Einsatzgruppen* (special units) degraded, tortured, and humiliated human beings are the result of their own merciless, brutal upbringing. Only people who have personally experienced emotional and physical cruelty and disrespect as children can pass on such contempt for human dignity and can even carry it out with gloating pleasure. This idea about the presumed right of superior people to eliminate others was not only narcissistic but also infantile and violently revengeful.

It was paramount for the Germans to find a scapegoat onto which all their feelings of self-hatred and impotence could be projected. The Jews were not really the cause of the raging spite and mistrust but the instrument for its relief. Provide any group of prejudiced people filled with self-hatred and fear with a special minority target and the results will be devastating. And if, as in Auschwitz, a scapegoat people have already been presented to their torturers as prisoners, as dangerous enemies, and as inferior, worthless life, few will have a conflict of conscience while killing.

"We thought that only criminals or other dangerous groups of people went to the camps," many Germans would say when they heard about torture and killing and when they recalled seeing wretched-looking people in striped prison uniforms, all without being particularly alarmed. But does it make any difference whether one is tortured or killed because one is a Jew, a Pole, a homosexual, a Communist, or even a criminal? How many different possibilities of interpretation are left when you see inhuman treatment? A person observes, judges, and decides. Cognizance is a decision and that decision reflects one's conscience. And the Germans' incognizance—whether due to mental laziness, blind belief, or looking the other way—is part of their guilt.

A mass execution of the dimensions of the concentration-camp gassing, which was certainly known by large portions of the German people, is only possible if there is a common denominator: consent.

The logical conclusion from all the excuses is that no matter what the *Reichsbürger* saw and heard, there was absolutely nothing that would have moved most of them to be alarmed, to question, or to interfere. Later, when they learned what had taken place, they weren't even shocked about their ignorance but rather were perplexed about the incredibly shifty regime that had bluffed them. Yet did Hitler really demand more of them than they were willing to give? It couldn't have been only his magical dictatorship and irresistible orders that made innumerable individuals fulfill orders that made them personally guilty.

Not surprisingly, the Germans have never come to terms any more with their mighty Führer than with their mutual creation, the Third Reich. They still can't let go of Adolf Hitler: he's a comrade, a hated father, an admired brother. They lived with him for twelve intense years, shared profoundly tumultuous events with him, from glory to gore. His megalomaniacal face hung on almost everyone's living-room wall and his unsmiling presence graced many a bedside table. This intimate relationship—comparable to a tempestuous marriage that had ended in a violent and painful divorce—accounts for the troubling attachment the Germans still feel for him. No matter how traumatic a marriage might have been, how terrible and disappointing, some parts of it were once real, desired, and quite fulfilling.

Hitler is the man the Germans hate to hate. As a people, they have formed an unresolved, ambivalent, unbalanced relationship with the former dictator, who had represented (in a slightly exaggerated form) the German bourgeois and his secret dreams. Adolf Hitler acted out the citizen of the Reich's boldest narcissistic fantasies of omnipotence. But when he began to overact, the Germans grew irritated, then disappointed, and in the end very angry with him—not so much for having ruined their country as for making it close to impossible to keep idolizing and worshipping him without a conflict. He cheated the Germans out of the chance to cherish and celebrate him as a people's hero, and *that* was unforgivable. Instead of rewarding him with marble monuments and parks named after him they had to swallow their pride and degrade him to the status of a closet hero. Yet he is disturbingly immortal, which shows that evil is as inextinguishable as good, and his name still triggers about as many pros as cons among his contemporaries.

In the course of my conversations with older Germans, I never heard them express genuine shock about their own position during the Nazi years or self-criticism at being drawn so deeply in without resistance.

But recognition and insight require humbleness and courage. Neither is quintessentially German. The German is courageous only when fulfilling an order as perfectly as possible. It has been a favorite protective excuse that resisting an order resulted inevitably in draconic punishment, including death, but there are no records that confirm that speculation. On the other hand, why would they refuse orders when order fulfillment was of the highest priority all their lives and when they had no inner independence or strength?

Indeed, as much as the Germans liked to organize everything from humor to mass murder, they could not be found in overabundance in organized resistance. Resistance develops from an inner, concrete desire for freedom at any cost and from the instinctive impulse to defend it whenever it is attacked. These, however, are not German ideals. Rather, to carry out orders, to obey, to submit to authority is part of the freedom of a proud citizen. It is rewarding to serve the current "Führer." A lack of solidarity, loyalty, and spontaneity makes the German an opponent of resistance.

Yet spontaneous resistance and acts of civil courage did occur, and the people who helped untiringly, even risked their lives in these attempts simply to behave as human beings, would resent being seen as particularly brave. How far from grace must a people have fallen if ordinary gestures by a few become landmark humanitarian acts and cruelties daily routines. A gift of a piece of bread, a smile in public, a word of encouragement had to be considered heroic, and the ones who didn't do anything viewed themselves after the war as selfless people if they didn't tell the Gestapo where the Jews were still hiding. If every German had displayed just a modicum of courage, a tiny contribution to decency, then together they could have created a climate of solidarity that might have prevented what happened.

When I was looking for people to talk to, I was also looking for strong emotions which I considered to be only natural—like outrage, sorrow, and remorse. I had never before heard older Germans explicitly express genuine distress about their Nazi past, but I thought it had to be hidden somewhere. They must have questioned themselves, God, humanity. They must have damned the fate that swept a man like Hitler onto their shores, cursed their parents for having raised them at the altar of obedience, hated the people who killed so many in their name, hated themselves if they did the killing. But the Germans are not given to irrational outbursts of passion that would disturb the regimented soul system. The German soul wears a uniform.

In the landmark book *The Inability to Mourn*, written in the mid-sixties by Margarethe and Alexander Mitscherlich, the authors hopefully concluded that "something has to give the Germans back the ability to mourn." Twenty years later, I could only come to the discouraging conclusion that this something has yet to be found.

They are still unable to mourn. I sat in their living rooms, listened to their recollections and ruminations, and felt a chill. Their eyes were cold and apathetic; their voices, like my father's, reportorial when they spoke of carnage and calm consciences. They were like impersonators whose performance showed some skill but was essentially hollow, with all feeling cut off. But repressed memories are not forgotten memories—a few scratches are sufficient and all kinds of conflicting emotions erupt. But the memories remain uninvestigated. These people are too old to risk the danger of opening their shrunken hearts, letting that stream of multi-layered, unresolved feelings flow. Then they would have to start from scratch, work through their past, and question the last forty or fifty years. But their time is up, they can't go back.

Another baffling characteristic of this generation emerged: they have no interest in their own contemporaries. Despite their endless ravings about the "wonderful camaraderie" with their war buddies, these men don't seem to have formed genuine relationships with them. They shared so much, yet the war failed to unite them. There was no growing political awareness, no desire to fight for a better future. Being back among the living left these survivors with one obvious conclusion: never stick your neck out again for a single person, cause, or ideology. Their curiosity extinguished, they are afraid to open up, to be enthusiastic, or to take a stand. The Third Reich has left a joyless people without orientation, bitter about the past and worried about the future.

On one level I felt sad when I recognized the brutality of a dictatorship that worked like a stencil, leaving behind deprived, depressed cutouts who had lost their emotions and their conscience all along the bloody tracks. On the other hand, listening to these somehow remarkable, stubborn, ignorant, and resilient warriors who had so much endurance and so little compassion made me angry over and over again. Among the thousands of sentences peppered with phrases such as "I didn't do anything," "How about the Russians?" and "But there were many good things too," the words "pain," "loss," "shame," "remorse," and "pity" appeared in few vocabularies. "That business with the Jews shouldn't have happened" was usually the most engaged form of contrition.

As much as I had given up on the Germans, once in a while a miracle unfolded over coffee and cookies: I met people who had hated the Nazis and had seen right through them, even if they couldn't stop their country's delirious downhill race. The difference between the average and the outstanding was remarkable, from a delightful, feisty Communist hairdresser to a soulful concentration-camp survivor, several organized anti-Fascists, and a handful of wise, reflective men, all still alert, engaged, and uncompromising. These courageous, rare individuals kept the almost extinguished flame of hope flickering for me. And it is because of their mere existence that I emerged bruised but in one piece from my dive into the abyss called fatherland.

I suspect that the Germans' mistrust is based not only on their feelings of betrayal by their Führer but also on their confusion deep down about their peculiar fate of staying alive while others had to die. Why did *they* live? If there was justice, the oppressed would deserve to survive, not their oppressors, and the Germans comprehend in a primitive way that their survival is a totally undeserved, irrational gift one should seize greedily and hold on to without asking any questions. In a generous, compassionate human being, the fact of survival by luck would elicit sorrow for the less fortunate ones, but not in the Germans. It is in their uncharitable nature that they can't go beyond their own pain and reach out to their victims.

The Germans never paid a tribute to suffering; they came up with money instead. Although the German government still pays restitution sums, this reparation to Jews resembles in its administrative style the once efficient killing of the very same people. Bureaucrats once again wrestle with numbers and files and lack emotional identification with the victims, but today their task is to ascertain just how severe the "damage" is if a human being has been persecuted and imprisoned for racial reasons: "Which concentration camp were you in? Can you prove just how *much* you suffered?"

Jean Améry, the Austrian philosopher and Auschwitz survivor, who killed himself in 1978, wrote: "Anyone who has suffered torture never again will be able to be at ease in the world, the abomination of the annihilation is never extinguished." If Jewish concentration-camp survivors had to live with their memories of degradation, torture, and humiliation and could die of sadness and heartbreak, why didn't this happen to the Germans as well? How did they shrug it off? Did they feel superior even in suffering?

The truth is, the Germans have remained tortured too —as they should as oppressors—because what they've committed is an irrevocably guilty act. They haven't survived the cold-blooded annihilation of other people without substantial psychological damage—but they are not aware of it. With every single extinguished life, something in the murderers died with the murdered in the trenches, gas chambers, and ovens. The smoke that blew from the chimneys of the death camps was mixed with a substance that was extricated from the guilty and will remain missing for as long as they live, denying them what they so vehemently searched for after the war: peace and happiness.

# 10

## *Pink Rabbit Slippers*

How did it all start? How do love affairs start? A glimpse of something unfathomable yet clamorously desired that takes your breath away. I still think it was the pink rabbit slippers that made me fall in love with America.

"Pink rabbit slippers?" comes the puzzled reply, and I add, still with a sense of pride, "I grew up with packages from America." Those heavy brown boxes from a dreamland far, far away, often torn from a bumpy trip on a freighter, have shaped my childhood as much as did the ruins and cripples of my native land. For me, those boxes were a symbol of freedom and superiority. Whatever my inestimable Lithuanian-American aunts sent, used or new, edible or wearable, every little item was a precious gift, a ray of hope for a child living in the country of shattered faith and ragged clothes. But more than just material treasures, they reached out through the spirit of giving and made me feel special. A country that was inhabited by such generous people who sent wonderful presents to two little

German girls they had never met had to be paradise. I was overwhelmed with gratitude and affection and became hopelessly infatuated with America.

Decades later, in 1982, I went to see one aunt, Barbara, for the first and last time, together with my mother, who was visiting from Majorca. I finally met the crucial but somehow anonymous link to my adopted country but was saddened when she turned out to be over eighty and senile. We repeatedly tried to tell her who we were—I in English, my mother in Lithuanian—but Aunt Barbara kept the faraway look in her eyes and started to chatter in her native tongue. I was close to tears because I couldn't show her my delayed gratitude for all those packages she had sent to Germany. It was a moving event. Three generations from two different countries, all of them immigrants now living on two different continents, were gathered in a modest, middle-class home in Connecticut, trying to connect Germany, Lithuania, and America.

Barbara's daughter brought out an old box filled with photographs of my young father and my sister and me, from around 1949–50, some of which I had never seen before. My mother, like all proud mothers and wives, had sent proof of her happiness to America a long time ago. I picked out my favorite one, which showed my sister and me cuddled up on one big chair, giggling, and pointed out to my aunt which one I was. She smiled and I think she suddenly knew—at least that's what I want to believe.

To this day, the Germans' gratitude and admiration for their supportive "big brother" has never faded. After the war ended, the Americans were popular winners, friendly, handsome, and good-natured. No Ally was nicer and more forgiving than the smiling guys in uniform who so generously distributed chewing gum, nylons, and Camels among the ravenous population. While all the other Allied forces never quite warmed up to the Germans and found it hard to forget their crimes, the easygoing Americans were neither reserved nor overly judgmental. They mingled with the Germans and dated the *Fräuleins*, who were delighted and honored to go out with, or even marry, a real Ami. This indestructible bond of good fellowship set the tone for the decades to follow, and both the Nazi generation and their offspring became devoted followers of anything American.

The postwar generation, moreover, was thirsting for something untainted and fresh to relieve the burden of war, shame, and Nazism, but postwar Germany offered nothing worth copying. We had to build our future, our role models, and our dreams from scratch, and for inspiration we looked as far away from the homeland as we could. For me, ideas about freedom were closely connected to the wish to be free of the German stigma. I felt like a spiritual orphan who had put herself up for mental adoption. I was looking for something better, I wanted to be more than just an ordinary German girl, for I was certain that otherwise nobody would ever accept me, because nobody likes Germans.

But America meant first and foremost pop culture and consumerism, and I found it inconceivable to associate this fanciful, happy Shangri-la with anything serious or cerebral; it was not the country of poets and thinkers. Everything I had learned about America was from movies, music, and magazines. America was like a sumptuous photo album come alive, with sounds, colors, and images all melted together into a country so big, brash, and diverse that everything and everybody seemed to fit in seamlessly. From Huckleberry Finn and Jayne Mansfield, Goofy and the Grand Canyon, to Tiny Tim and Charles Manson.

But for me, the most important images from America

were the movies, compared to which the reality of postwar Germany was no match. Long before we had TV (around 1959) and I could watch on Saturdays *Father Knows Best* and *Mr. Ed*, I had discovered Cowboys and Indians in Cinemascope at the huge movie theaters in my neighborhood. My passion for movies reached its peak around 1955, when I was nine, and every Sunday I ran to the Thalia or the Harmony and stood in line with hundreds of jittery kids, peeking with barely contained excitement at the colorful poster that announced the movie of the afternoon. I must have seen every single Western that was made in the fifties. Because of the national slim pickings we were bombarded with B Western and Adventure imports from America. One look at German movie stars was sufficient to understand why Jeff Chandler appeared to be a distinguished actor with dazzling charm and Rhonda Fleming a matchless beauty.

After the tenth cowboy film, I knew the Wild West as intimately as my way to school and had figured out that life in Laramie and Dodge City, while more enthralling, was as predictable as life in a German suburb. The heroes were mostly played by James Stewart, Rory Calhoun, Rock Hudson, and Richard Widmark, all of whom I liked very much, and yet somehow I was saddled more often than not with Audie Murphy or Randolph Scott, both of whom I couldn't stand.

The Indians—or "Redskins," as they were called—were an interesting bunch whom I couldn't quite place, but I didn't think it strange that the Cowboys wanted to kill them all, because they were dangerous savages who raped blond pioneer women, scalped white men, and set farms on fire. They wanted rifles and firewater and spoke broken English, so they must have been foreigners. Judging from Audie's fierce glance and serious warnings, these racial misfits had to be eradicated from the American prairie for good. It never occurred to me then that the Indians might be real people who belonged in that country more than Audie Murphy did. I thought they were invented by Hollywood.

My entire life as a teenager and part of my adolescence was affected by the desire to shed, inside and out, what was visibly German about me. Many characteristics could be shed, softened, filed off a little—except for one thing: the language. The native tongue was treacherous and always gave away the secret. When I was twelve, I had an American pen pal who lived in Cleveland. I had polished my school English by singing along with American hit songs on the BBC, and was therefore able to beg Raymond for a record that had cast a spell on me the minute I had heard it on the radio. Weeks later—this must have been in 1958—I received my first record. It was a single called "Wake Up, Little Susie," by the Everly Brothers, who sounded simply revolutionary to me. A round black disc symbolized my linguistic independence.

It didn't matter that we didn't have a record player; what counted was the possession. I then began to collect idols and built an altar for all of them. They were sacred treasures and subjected to a strict nationality code. The worshipped gods had to be foreigners, primarily Americans. That was my private "denazification"—and my revenge against what I considered "typically German." I don't know how many hundreds of times I said those words throughout the years, but it wasn't a joyous exclamation or meant as a seal of approval for outstanding achievements. On the contrary. This phrase, uttered with utmost contempt, was used liberally for characterizing anything from abominable, thin-lipped behavior by grown-ups to the "cultural" transgressions that sent shock waves down my spine.

It isn't too hard to imagine what the German *Kultur* must have been like after twelve years of unwarrantable bad taste and a crash art diet ordered by a moronic dictator. Many talented artists left relatively quickly after 1933, and after the war most didn't want to come back, and who could blame them? They had been in the prime of their careers when they left, and they had adapted, more or less successfully, to the new culture in those foreign countries that had allowed them greater freedom.

The young artists and entertainers who remained after the war had started their careers under Hitler, and they lacked the desire to create independent work, to experiment, or to test their craft. They became the third-rate pop-music lyricists and singers, film directors and lackluster film stars who mercilessly inflicted themselves on a culture-damaged Germany in the fifties. There was nothing incongruous about it, though, because they had an appreciative mass audience—the former Hitler Youth and other younger inhabitants of Nazi Germany who had never known any artistic expression devoid of the National Socialist idea and therefore couldn't make comparisons.

Germany's idea of escaping the harsh struggle of daily life was through movies of unprecedented triteness. A favorite was a sort of German Hillbilly-Western that featured a loden-clad, kindhearted forester who had to deal in his own exemplary way with the pitfalls and joys associated with this thrilling, profoundly German profession. Food for thought was not what the population stood in line for, and the few feature films about the war were battle epics that showed soldiers at work in Russia.

Popular music was no better in the fifties. Jovial middle-aged gentlemen in suits and ties, with neatly parted hair and catchy names like Freddy, Heinz, and Rudi, warbled the world's greatest banalities in monotonous voices, often accompanied by an accordion. The female entertainers, often named Lolita, Friedel, and Margot, were maternal and middle-aged as well and dressed in dirndls. Occasionally, though, they wore racy robes with mink stoles and sang pluckily about *Weltschmerz*. And seeing them assembled on German TV variety shows, standing there like wooden cutouts singing little ditties with vacuous smiles, I knew that this assault on the ears and eyes was the delayed revenge of the Third Reich.

I needed to get out of that cultural prison and longed for a musical key that would unlock my smoldering lust for emotional pandemonium. I wanted color, imagination, fantasy, and dazzling, daring, hot sounds that would make my legs and arms shake. And I got it from the land that knows a girl's heart. Rock 'n' roll set my soul and ears on fire, and instantly I became a rock-crazed teenage slave, mostly because of *him*. Elvis. He was the rocking knight in tight pants who sang with his velvety, insinuating voice irritating songs like "Won't You Wear My Ring Around Your Neck?"— another record that Raymond had sent me—with such trembling passion that I forgot to wonder what the words even meant.

However, Elvis's pedestal began to shake when he joined the Army and was stationed in Germany. With his cropped brown hair and dull uniform he lost all his magic and rebelliousness—and his Americanism. And yet Elvis in Germany, singing, as a little homage to his host country, "*Muss I denn zum Städtele hinaus*," was a perfect metaphor for the deep, ingratiating German-American friendship—except that I thought he was a traitor and a fake.

Periodically, my interest in and identification with America went beyond movie stars and music because to me even politics looked better "over there." John F. Kennedy, not Adenauer, was my idea of a modern politician, and that he was a Berliner by his own admission endeared him even more to me, even though I was a Hamburger. And when Kennedy died, my tears were as real as when Martin Luther King died, which was strange in a way, because my life was as devoid of blacks as it was of Jews.

Yet while I was still dreaming about America my sister Sylvie got lucky. Almost as infected with the American bacillus as I was, in 1962 she was shipped off to New York for a year to become an "au pair" for a German-American family in Farmingdale, Long Island.

"My sister is in America," I would say in school, and it sounded so continental. "Ooh, really?" my friends would sigh, and we were envious that she was so much closer to our idols than we were. Soon, the letters started coming in and they smelled of the brave new world. She lived near the beach, the family had a boat, and she could go to New York once or twice a week; the people were the greatest in America and she never wanted to come back. After a few months she started casually strewing little English words and phrases throughout her letters, like "never mind" or "anyway," and also enclosed some photos.

My envy soared. Sylvie at Jones Beach in a tiny, striped bikini, Sylvie in a bare-shouldered sundress at an art fair in Greenwich Village. I had never seen any of the clothes she was wearing—we had kept a tight watch over each other—and that made me nervous. America was a thief; it took away my sister, alienated her, inhabited her, changed and corrupted her. Her tone became even more cocky, almost condescending, as if she felt sorry for her peasant folks in quaint old Germany who had to live life without marshmallows—a nasty-sounding confection for all I cared.

Her life seemed like a string of dazzling events. She went to hear gospel songs in a Harlem church on Sunday and modern jazz in a downtown club on Friday. She raved about Saks Fifth Avenue and Woolworth's and Central Park, where she ate pretzels. She even managed to get herself invited to a debutante ball at the Waldorf-Astoria, and my mother, who already saw her being chased by a prince brandishing the other glass slipper, made her a beaded white evening gown, which I had to model and which was sent by airmail to Long Island.

When Sylvie returned by ship I could only stare at her and swallow hard. She actually chewed gum and said "Hi," which I thought was affected, and shook her new platinum-blond tresses. Her long legs were partly covered with a shrill flower-print garment of unknown origin. "Bermuda shorts," she explained, and when my gaze wandered down to her feet in white canvas, she said matter-of-factly, "Keds."

Her luggage was out of this world—a hard, fire-red suitcase with a matching cosmetics case. "Samsonite. Great, isn't it?" she said nonchalantly. I was quiet and felt like a hick. She had left as a dark-blond, shy, gawky teenager of nineteen and returned a sophisticated woman of the world. So it was true. America makes a star out of everyone.

For the next few weeks my mother and I hung on her every word, but her suitcase and its contents were more riveting. It was like our childhood again, with our version of America compressed into items, this time items purchased by a German teenager. There were records by Peter, Paul and Mary and Dave Brubeck, Levi's for me, several Brooks Brothers cotton shirts, candies with a hole in the middle, white socks, piles of cosmetics, and a surprising amount of aspirin. The secret of Sylvie's blondness was a certain Miss Clairol and her deep tan was protected by Coppertone.

When she tried to enrich our palates by introducing pancakes with sausages, we protested such shenanigans and also forbade her to serve everything with melted cheese. But after the canned pineapple casserole, topped with toothachingly sweet meringue, we began to lose faith in the United States. After the summer, though, everything went back to normal and America was put back into perspective. Only an empty blue jar of Noxzema placed visibly on the shelf in the bathroom reminded our family that one of us had actually crossed the Atlantic.

My first trip to America took place ten years later after a new era had started. I had met a few visiting American hippies in my commune and had liked them very much. The irreverent Robert Crumb, a much-treasured chronicler of American life among hip Germans, had given me hysterical new insights about an America that had little in common with movie glamour or with Norman Rockwell's charming world. I was eager to go there and track down the cartoon characters Leonore Goldberg, Mr. Natural, and Fritz the Cat. So I went in the summer of 1972, only to be suspected of reactionary tendencies because in the socially conscious circles I was part of, imperialistic America was out and the spiritualistic Far East was in.

Visiting America was like making a personal appearance at the scene of my beloved childhood memories, and I tried to connect fiction and truth. I traveled with a friend cross-country from New York to California, driving and hitchhiking, and it was a wonderful, illuminating trip. Coming from a country that offers mostly hostility toward unruly travelers, I was deeply impressed by the Americans; their generosity, warmth, and openness toward strangers were nothing less than a revelation.

We were smiled at, picked up, and brought home by truck drivers, students, and free spirits. I never had any idea that so many Americans, including highway patrolmen, had been stationed in Germany or had relatives with German roots; I began to think that they were just trying to be polite. They all seemed to be impressed with Germany and I felt relieved.

Driving along America's highways, stopping in small towns, staying in drive-in motels, tasting greasy food in sleazy diners, and having picnics in breathtaking natural settings, I got a sense of the soul of America. But what was really mind-boggling was that America was everything I had imagined it would be, as if this country had set out to indulge me by preserving everything from the last twenty-five years that I had come to classify as "typically American." They were actually alive, the freckled little kids with flattops, jeans, and high-top sneakers and the old farmers wearing overalls, plaid wool shirts, and baseball caps. New York's fading East Side beauties with smeared ruby lipstick and blue hair under dainty hats were no movie walk-ons, and San Francisco's hippies with ponytails and bell-bottoms, saying "peace" with dreary smiles, were still on the streets. It was a great satisfaction for me to revel in my American stereotypes, saving the discovery of the minds inside the clothes for later.

That time came three years later when I came to New York prepared to stay if I liked it enough. I think the reason I came to America might indeed have been to fulfill a childhood dream, but the answer to the other, more important question, "Why did you leave Germany?" is quite different.

I was running away from a father figure and a fatherland, and America helped me carry out the escape. Wanting to leave Germany meant wanting to free myself from that sticky legacy; this had always been a subconscious desire, almost a logical conclusion to the distressing facts and negative image I had to face about my homeland, and the question wasn't so much "if" it would happen as "when."

America was a natural choice for my new identity because, strangely enough, I knew it much better than Germany. I had never had any desire to travel in Germany and sample larger doses of people I couldn't stand. The Rhine, the Black Forest, medieval towns, and lederhosen-wearing folks were as strange to me as to a first-time tourist.

Until 1975, when I was twenty-nine, I tried to live in Germany the only way I thought was possible for a mistrusting, critical, and angry descendant of the Nazi generation, and that meant searching for values and worthy causes outside of Germany. It was a life without an inner home, or *Heimat*, without a haven or a harbor. Adventuress, vagabond, homeless cosmopolitan—that's how I saw myself. Besides, it was also a flattering female image of strength and independence.

My sense of mental dislocation, uprootedness, and isolation grew mostly out of this lack of belonging. I didn't have a clan or a political and psychological climate that nurtured and protected me. The extension of a family is the country, a nationality that can offer emotional stability and a sense of identity even when family ties have been severed. But I couldn't separate the country from the people; they were welded together. So I abandoned them both.

Living in a foreign country, however, evoked feelings that I had rarely experienced inside Germany—shame and, occasionally, a trace of guilt. In America I was without the protective armor of being among one's own people; I couldn't disappear into the masses or hide behind the language. What I could sustain easily in Germany, the sense of being innocent and the knowledge that everybody around me knew that I was guiltless, crumbled before my eyes. I felt like a walking question mark, a person who must prove her innocence. But in reality, it seems that the only person who had a problem with being German was me.

How did they see me? Who did they think I was? A typical German, practically a descendant of Adolf Hitler? I've often been told that I'm a combative troublemaker, but I always considered this a compliment—ample evidence of having escaped the obedient, authority-loving German character. And when a tall, red-haired Texan in New York introduced me as "This is Bini, she takes no shit," I was pleased.

The Americans were big-hearted, tolerant hosts who embraced any stranger regardless of his or her race, creed, or past. Nobody ever asked me how I felt about being German or how much I knew about the Nazis. And why should they have? I was evidently an upstanding person who condemned her own country for all the right reasons and who wasn't to blame for old war crimes. It was only after living in America for seven years that I began to consider whether the Americans ever wondered what my parents did in the war.

It had never occurred to me before how strange the lack of curiosity and the apparent absence of judgment were. But deep down I felt that they perceived and treated me exactly the same way I related to older Germans, as a person whose handicap is kindly overlooked. Maybe they didn't want to hurt my feelings by bringing up my family's Nazi past, the only kind of past they could imagine for the parents of a German daughter who was born in 1946. For to this day, Germany and the Germans are emotionally judged by the Nazi past. After more than fifty years, most people have become comfortable with this prejudice; it's widely accepted and rarely evokes stern criticism or repudiation. Nazis and Germans are now as inseparable as Astaire and Rogers.

"They weren't all Nazis?" asks a forty-year-old highly educated American editor, with a soupçon of disappointment. Wouldn't it be easy if all Germans were once Nazis, are still Nazis? Easy to judge, easy to condemn, nothing complicated, just black and white. It's such a convenient box and all Germans fit in. I know from my own experience that my extremely narrow views of Germany were as prejudiced as could be, maintained by the refusal to deal with the issues and let go of the box. Others, too, show great resistance to revising their image of Germany. While a lot of Americans fear that Germany might still be the same, they also find it comforting to assume it. Using recent German history as the epitome of evil is always uplifting for other countries, for their wars and atrocities always pale in comparison with Germany's.

Blondes might have more fun in the movies, but being a blond German counteracts that blessing which supposedly gets you diamonds and lusty proposals from rich men. It got me nothing but tiring routines. But I used to laugh along when Americans thought the most hysterical bit of ethnic fun was to yell "*Jawohl*" or "*Heil Hitler,*" arm raised, in a high-pitched military voice, in the middle of an otherwise cultivated conversation.

Nobody understood better than I how deeply the irrepressible Nazi caricature had penetrated the layers of human brain tissue that store stereotypes, and how irresistible such distinctive images are for jokers. But over the years I

stopped laughing and started to get angry and annoyed, all
to no avail, for I was up against the century's classic of evil.
Wanting to beautify the ugly German comes close to wanting to repackage the devil himself by sawing off his horns,
throwing away his pitchfork, and putting him in a fancy
designer coat, unaware that the tip of his tail still peeks out.
The audience boos; they want their old, familiar devil back.

"What do you think when you think of Germany?" I
asked American friends, and strangers as well. The answers
formed an eclectic catalogue of the best and the worst of
the twentieth century. Hitler, Einstein, Goethe and Gör-
ing, Wagner and *Würstchen*, Mercedes and Marx, Bach and
Mozart, Beckmann and Eichmann, Heinrich Heine and
Heinrich Himmler, Riefenstahl, Fritz Lang, and Marlene
Dietrich, Bauhaus, Brecht, and Bergen-Belsen, Heidelberg
and Heidegger, *The Threepenny Opera* and Six-Million-Jews
Blues. Auschwitz.

The damage was done a long time ago. A nation trampled
over its legendary achievements and left a wasteland. Nobody *loves* Germany, is enchanted by it, finds it irresistible,
or is driven to impassioned hymns about its playful charm,
magical spirit, and raucous zest. Respect, definitely; admiration, yes; a strange fascination, for sure; and a big hand
for its remarkable economic productivity. But never love.
You love Paris (not even the French can diminish that) or
Rome and the Italians, but Germany leaves you strangely
uncomfortable and unmoved, it doesn't have a soul that is
easy to like—or see. "It's beautiful," you might say, "the
forests, the romantic villages, the art treasures." Physical
beauty, preserved by meticulous minds. But who would
ever mention the inner beauty of the common older German
of today? Does it even exist?

America, by contrast, is a lovable country with lovable

people. I instantly liked their bright-eyed congeniality and casual warmth—a little bit like overgrown, playful children who have the attention span of a lightning bolt. I couldn't help comparing the German soul with the American spirit and seeing melancholy vs. bluster, fatalism vs. optimism, crippling mistrust vs. blind faith. Germans are prickly diggers, complicated, uneasy; Americans are butterflies, graceful ice skaters who glide away when the polite chitchat is exhausted.

I always envied Americans for what was for me unabashed, flag-waving patriotism, and I wished that I could feel just a tiny bit of it for Germany. I was often envious of other nationalities, of people my age who didn't have to feel discomfort when delving into their country's past and were not silenced by a hasty "We didn't know what was going on." A proud Spaniard, Briton, or American is the norm, but a proud German?

I remember the 1960 Olympic Games in Rome. Germany won so many gold medals. The achievements of handsome and wholesome-looking young German athletes were admirable—and record-breaking, even—but I dreaded the moment when the medals were to be awarded in that uncomfortable ceremony of raising flags and playing national anthems. "Deutschland, Deutschland über Alles"—officially, the words weren't allowed anymore after the war—filled the huge stadium. Was I the only one who felt a sudden chill, a short moment of embarrassment, and this strange feeling of not being able to enjoy or trust outstanding acts that were tied to nationalities—not even in sports?

No victories after the war have been sweet. Many times, when something German was singled out positively, when someone German won an award, achieved fame, set a record, I always thought, "They don't deserve it. It's not real."

My own resentment might have been stronger than that of foreigners but this contradictory quality always puzzled me. How can bad people be so good?

Few Americans would ever separate or disassociate from their country. Not only do Americans love their country with the passion of a protective parent, but many cannot even consider the possibility that other humane and egalitarian forms of society might exist in other countries.

I have seen some of the finest, most critical minds fidgeting in their chairs and losing their equilibrium in conversations where a foreigner pointed out some less than wonderful development in America. Their only response seems to be the sly "Why are you here, then?" Not to mention the defiant "Love it or leave it" advice—the ideological twin brother of Germany's "If you don't like it here, why don't you go to East Germany?"—that was thrown my way a few times in the States.

One doesn't have to be a German who mistrusts patriotism to feel at times alarmed by the pounding, nationalistic slogans in the media that propagate global Americanism and assure the citizens that everybody will be happy if they firmly believe in American values. All this has an edge of severe incertitude and I have yet to understand what it is that urges celebrities, politicians, and the "man in the street" to declare publicly, out of the blue, that they are "proud to be an American" and that "this is the greatest country in the world." Which deep doubts are being expressed here and which issues masked? What is patriotism worth if it's nothing more than a fearful turning inward, blocking out challenge and inspiration, a substitute for lives devoid of meaning? Is this a Band-Aid patriotism for the recent self-inflicted wounds of a country that once thought of itself as invulnerable, innocent, and pure?

It came as a surprise to me to discover that mainstream America is credulous and alarmingly undereducated—even more so given its status as the prime media nation of the world which not only makes the news but breaks it too. They are rarely forced to adjust, to excel, or to survive on any terms but their own, whether linguistically or culturally. There are few large areas left on this planet that haven't been saturated with American ideas instilling the wondrous, insatiable desire for Coca-Cola, big bucks, and soap operas.

I don't expect Americans to know as much about Germany as I know about America, but I do expect them to want to know. Their current condemnation of an image exclusively attached to one country distracts them from gaining a broader view. Indeed, Hitler was an evil man and the Germans responsible for his rise, but why restrict the evil to him? It would be better for everyone, Americans too, to know the dangers of dictatorship, Fascism, racism, and genocide. If you want to judge us by our past, know our past.

For years I kept a low profile in certain areas and phrased criticism only with utmost care when I touched on subjects like wars, countries, guilt, and complicity. Many saw it as natural that I had feelings of shame and sadness, but I rarely heard more than the expression of detached shock from others, although I felt that the killing of millions of Jews was reason for mourning for everyone. Sometimes when I struggled through an explanation of why I feel so pained about the past, people looked at me with the warm sympathy of those who don't understand entirely but who think that they're thousands of miles removed. I wasn't looking for volunteers to come to my aid and relieve me of irksome feelings, I just longed to share the loss. But it seems that the roles of the innocent and the guilty were permanently assigned a long time ago.

I had never heard of the detention camps for Japanese in sunny California until a few years ago. It isn't a subject that is persistently crammed down one's throat by individuals or the media. It is unfortunate that one has to develop a hunter's instinct and the perseverance of an archaeologist to acquire more than cursory information about unpopular and pain-inducing historical events anywhere. It was disturbing to learn that my beloved America had formed an alliance with such terrible acts.

Naturally, I could relate very well to other people's lack of curiosity and knowledge about certain parts of their history. My American contemporaries must also have been subtly manipulated, or maybe just discouraged from asking questions about the wars in which their fathers had participated. I discovered that American dads didn't like to talk about World War II any more than their German counterparts did—and they were the winners. I haven't met many younger Americans who know specifically what their fathers experienced on the shores of Europe and the Pacific, at the gates of concentration camps, or up in the sky, bombing Germany, Hiroshima and Nagasaki—nor are they hell-bent to find out. What did the American fathers who liberated concentration camps tell their daughters and sons, wives and grandchildren? They must have seen more unforgettable sights than most people, including Germans, ever saw. It seems that wars are only alive while they last; once they find their bitter end on the outside, the pain goes underground and the battles rage on in memory. Perhaps if our fathers had kept the horror alive and skipped the glory, we might better understand the uselessness of wars.

Many Americans still cling to an often heroic and romantic view of World War II, the war that was a "good war" because the world was liberated from Hitler's Fascism and because the Americans could act out one of their favorite fantasies—coming to the aid of the enslaved and the downtrodden and restoring order, peace, and justice. But because the Americans have always fought their battles outside of their homeland so that there would never be bombs over Tennessee and rubble in Manhattan, they are unable to comprehend the traumatizing fear, anger, and helplessness of people standing by while one's home, one's hometown, and most of one's country are reduced to ruins by foreign bombing raids. Because buried under the piles of rubble that once were children's rooms, cozy kitchens, and lovingly tended gardens is not just the burned flesh of one's fellow citizens but also the very concept of being indestructible in the safety of one's home. The Germans were bombed out of their dreams and their presumption of innocence, and this vulnerability to arbitrary destruction has left them scarred and overcautious to this day.

My thirteen years in the United States have helped me change my attitudes toward both America and Germany. I adjusted my blind approval for everything American and my extreme hostility toward Germany. Moreover, I have begun to understand that my American adventure also served a higher purpose; I was seeking closeness through distance. Actually, I needed to work on reconciliation with Germany.

I watched my native land from afar, though with some trepidation, and I was proud to be of the same nationality as Heinrich Böll, Rainer Werner Fassbinder, Joseph Beuys. I read encouraging and praising words in the media about the thriving art scene and the reawakening of democratic instincts, poignantly demonstrated by the anti-nuclear movement and the pro-environmentalist Green Party. And yet these German achievements still get mixed reviews in America, with suspicion sprinkled amidst the reluctant recognition and approval.

What do they suspect? That the Führer might make a clandestine comeback in a modern disguise? That a new generation of Nazi-indoctrinated Germans might decide overnight to overthrow the democratic government and form a Fourth Reich? When will Germans finally be able to meet foreigners who don't have Nazis on their minds and suspicion in their hearts?

From what I hear, an awful lot of people avoid Germany while traveling through Europe. It is the country to pass up or pass through, maybe sampling a view of an old castle, a *Schweinshaxe* decorated with sauerkraut en route, or, even bolder, risking a two-day visit hiking up a mountain. For many foreigners a whole country full of Germans conjures up latent Teutonophobia and the clacking sound of marching jackboots, which strikes a panicky chord.

Nevertheless, those who admire and are captivated by recent cultural achievements and brave enough to visit a complicated, sundered country are favorably impressed. There is always an element of surprise mixed with the praise, as if it was expected that Nazis, disguised as ordinary citizens, would round up all foreigners who refused to drink beer and—with the help of barking German shepherds of course—transport them to an armed retraining camp. If one tries to dig deeper and pin down what exactly is expected of Germany today, the answers are as vague as all preconceived ideas are when under scrutiny. "I don't know," say some, "Germany doesn't seem very attractive." "I have no connection to it," say others. All add, a touch apologetically, "And the Holocaust, of course." Of course.

"You don't have an American passport?" Incredulity and raised eyebrows from the Americans I meet. "When are you getting one?" What's wrong with me? I live in America long enough to get an American passport and pass up this chance to cover up my real nationality and rid myself of its burden? A German not desperately seizing the offered protection? Maybe I'm just being "typically German"—stubborn, lead-footed, difficult. I once might have wanted it very badly, but I no longer want to exchange this admittedly horrible green booklet for a slicker-looking blue one, because it means nothing to me. I'm half German by birth and fully German by legacy. For nothing in the world would I relinquish this nationality which has forced me to make crucial psychological excavations and has made me struggle so much. I'm not proud to be a German, and I wouldn't be proud to be an American. Too much national pride distracts from making essential discoveries.

"Do you miss Germany? Are you homesick sometimes?" I'm often asked. "Homesick?" A short, cynical laugh. "For that I have to have a home first." Home is where I hang my hat. I have found several hat racks in my life, but a home? In America I'm not a visitor anymore, I'm a voluntary immigrant, a new form of an old German standard. And just as many Germans fled from Hitler fifty years ago, so did I. But he has caught up with me.

Homesick? Yes, for the sounds and smells of my childhood. I am homesick for my memories, not for my country. I am homesick for the America of the pink rabbit slippers and the packages, for rubble playgrounds, military-blanket coats, and the men on crutches who had returned from the war.

I am homesick for the language. I love the German language. She is the real *Heimat*; all others are adopted children

214 / *What Did You Do in the War, Daddy?*

who, at first glance, can easily be confused with one's own flesh and blood. Languages are beautiful bridges. They lead from one shore to the other.

And America? I love America the way an orphan loves his kindhearted foster parents and the first room of his own. Without reservations.